Everyone is talking about
The Frugal Entr ...

"It's smart to be thrifty. Whether you're a brand-new business owner or an old-timer like me, The Frugal Entrepreneur *can help you manage your time and money better. Spend a little time and money on this book so you can start saving both in your business."*

> — Barbara J. Winter
> Author, *Making a Living Without a Job*

*"*The Frugal Entrepreneur *is an excellent, hands-on guide for people who want to make the most of their time, energy, and money. Follow the tips in this action-ready guide to business succcess and you'll be working smarter than ever."*

> — Michael LeBoeuf
> Author, *Working Smart* and *The Perfect Business*

"Lonier has done it again! The Frugal Entrepreneur *is packed with practical money-saving ideas. It's a quick read with long-lasting benefits."*

> — Alice Bredin
> Author, *The Virtual Office Survival Handbook*

"This book has all the information I've had to learn by trial and error—presented in a concise, wise, insightful, and often irreverent manner. It's a definite must for your small business bookshelf."

> — Larry Roth
> Editor, *Living Cheap News*

Also by Terri Lonier

WORKING SOLO
The Real Guide to Freedom & Financial Success
with Your Own Business

WORKING SOLO SOURCEBOOK
Essential Resources for Independent Entrepreneurs

WORKING SOLO
Getting Started (audiotape program)

The Frugal Entrepreneur™

Creative Ways to Save Time, Energy & Money in Your Business

Terri Lonier

PORTICO
•PRESS•

THE FRUGAL ENTREPRENEUR
Creative Ways to Save Time, Energy & Money in Your Business
by Terri Lonier

PORTICO
•PRESS•

Portico Press   (914) 255-7165
PO Box 190   (914) 255-2116 (fax)
New Paltz, NY 12561   (800) 222-7656 (orders only)

portico@workingsolo.com (e-mail)
http://www.workingsolo.com (Internet)

Library of Congress Cataloging-in-Publication Data

Lonier, Terri.
    The Frugal Entrepreneur: Creative Ways to Save Time, Energy & Money in Your Business / by Terri Lonier
        p. cm.
        Includes index.
ISBN 1-883282-70-5   trade paper
1. Small business—Management. 2. Entrepreneurship—Management.
3. Self-employed—Management. I. Title.
HD62.7.L65   1996
658.022—dc20   96-67106

Distributed to the trade by Publishers Group West, (800) 788-3123

Printed in the United States of America
10 9 8 7 6 5 4 3 2 1

This book is dedicated to the spirit of Benjamin Franklin—author, publisher, inventor, philosopher, diplomat, humorist, kite flyer, and frugal business owner— which lives on inside every modern entrepreneur.

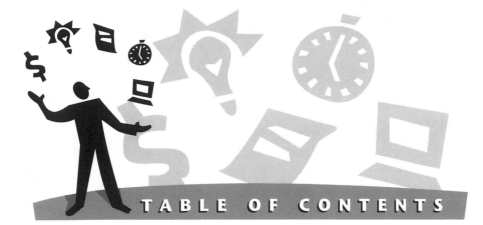

Forms • Peel and Stick • Fax or Mail? • Drop-Off Savings • Let
Them Ship It • Dumpster Diving • Peanuts, In and Out • Graded
Cartons • Cheaper Than Bubble Wrap • Tasty Protection • Online
Shipping Info

Chapter 7

Time Management 83

Activity vs. Achievement • List of Seven • Overlapping Plans •
Ease into Your Day • Measure Twice, Cut Once • End-of-Day
Closure • Know Your Bio-clock • Play to Your Strengths • Only
Value Need Apply • Outsource • Be a "Teflon" Delegator •
Magazine Management • Resource Routing • Stuffing on Hold •
Plan Your Errand Rounds • Line Sleuthing • Sign It by Stamp •
Small Is Beautiful • Master To-Do List • Rolodex Purge • Plan It! •
Slipping By Unnoticed • Important vs. Urgent • Bank Your Time •
To Meet or Not to Meet? • Agendas Steer the Course • The
Caffeine Helps, Too • Meeting Over the Wires

Chapter 8

Research 95

Start General, Not Specific • Bonus Books • Corporate Savings •
Directories on the Cheap • Recycled Media Directories • Research
Buddies • Avoid Expensive Detours on the Info Highway •
Searching with Sampler Hours • Digital Queries • Say Yahoo! •
Online Card Catalog • University Resources • Tape It • Join a
Control Group • Teach It and Reap • Office in a Briefcase

Chapter 9

Professional Advisors
& Associations 103

Your Personal Board of Directors • Advisors Worldwide • Their
Advice, Your Nickel • Thanks Year 'Round • The Power of
Association(s) • Small Print Says a Lot • Half-Year for Half Price •
Directory Deadlines • Power in Numbers • Have an Agenda •
Schedule Breathing Room • Time to Debrief • Capture "Keepers" •
Create an Action List • Name Badge on the Right • Power Partners
• Variety Is the Spice • Indirect Introductions

Foreword

It's time to explode the myths about frugality. When most people think about being frugal, they think about cutting back. But hardcore guerrilla marketers like myself know that's foolish economy. Thinking that stopping or decreasing your business activities can save money is a lot like thinking that stopping your watch can save time. Life doesn't work that way—particularly entrepreneurial life.

It's also time to shine a bright light on the old lie that time is money. Time is worth far more than money, especially to entrepreneurs. To the frugal business owner, time is a valuable ally. It brings patience and persistence into the scheme of things. It provides for balance in the life of the entrepreneur. It is, along with information, the currency of the coming century.

Today's entrepreneurs have more opportunities open to them than ever before. But the path is not without perils. Savvy entrepreneurs adopt the guerrilla's Golden Rule of making every investment pay off handsomely. They know that their enthusiasm about their business and their insights about their customers can be much more fruitful than mere dollars thrown at a solution.

Smart-thinking guerrilla entrepreneurs also pay ultra-close attention to details. They choose tools appropriate to their tasks and move easily between the old world of commonsense office operations and the new world of time- and money-saving technology. Above all, they never mistake efficiency for effectiveness.

Terri Lonier is a guerrilla marketer *par excellence*. Lucky for us, she also follows the guerrilla Golden Rule of creating alliances and sharing information. The result is this collection of invaluable and frugal tips guaranteed to save every entrepreneur time, energy, and money in their business. Its pages will puncture some entrepreneurial myths, put readers on the proper entrepreneurial road, and show budding and current practitioners of individual enterprise that it doesn't have to cost an arm and a leg to succeed in the entrepreneurial life.

It takes many years for most entrepreneurs to learn what is so comprehensively collected in this book. Alas, many of the entrepreneurial nuggets presented here usually are the results of painful trials and expensive errors. Terri gives us a shortcut past those trials and errors with her copious experience, her attention to tiny but nuclear-powered details, and her ability to tap the minds of entrepreneurs already out there in America, achieving big profits from their small businesses.

Best of all, this book presents its knowledge in a warm and engaging manner, peppered with examples, inspiration, good humor, and a sense of humanity that is so often absent from the world of business.

If you'd like a first-class ride to entrepreneurial success, while paying far less than the cost of a first-class ticket, you're in for a treat. *The Frugal Entrepreneur* can make you the *fulfilled* entrepreneur. That's exactly what Terri Lonier has in mind.

Jay Conrad Levinson
San Rafael, California

Jay Conrad Levinson is the author of the classic international bestseller *Guerrilla Marketing,* plus 18 other widely acclaimed books on business, careers, and time. His *Guerrilla Marketing* book series remains the top-selling marketing series of all time.

Introduction

Meet the frugal entrepreneur—dedicated to using creativity instead of cash to generate business success. These savvy individuals know the value of their time, energy, and money, and they spend each strategically to benefit their businesses.

And welcome to *The Frugal Entrepreneur,* a collection of practical tips and techniques that can help you make the most of your professional resources. Within these pages you'll find helpful ways to stretch your dollars, maximize your time, and optimize your energy as you create a successful enterprise.

The best practitioners of frugal entrepreneurship are not tightwads, bent on saving every cent. They know that while a penny saved is a penny earned, business success comes from more than adding up pennies. For example, you won't find these business owners spending time cutting up brown paper bags to create economical mailing envelopes. You will, however, find them recycling packing materials to save money and the environment. That's the focus of the material collected here: practical and useful without being outrageously penny-pinching. In other words, frugal with a view of the big picture.

When it comes to being masters of frugality, entrepreneurs know three important rules of success:

1. CHEAP CAN BE EXPENSIVE.

Savvy frugalists don't buy based on price, they *invest* based on *value.* They know that a quick, cheap solution may cost them more in the long run—when they'll be forced to make a replacement purchase or redo an action. The best frugal investments pay off over time.

2. TIME IS MORE VALUABLE THAN MONEY.

The most experienced frugal entrepreneurs know that time is their most valuable asset. They understand the limited nature of this resource: you can't make more, buy more, or even *steal* more. Entrepreneurs who manage their days, weeks, and months best are the ones who get twice as much done in the same allotted time. Fortunately for us, they're also the ones who have shared their techniques in this book.

3. LITTLE THINGS ADD UP.

While most frugal entrepreneurs aren't obsessed with micro-managing every penny of their business, they do sweat the details. They realize that a few dollars saved or wasted here and there can make a big difference in a company's bottom line at the end of the year. They understand the positive impact of time, energy, and money focused on the right target. They also recognize the value a single frugal idea can contribute to their business success.

Most of all, the frugal entrepreneurs I've met over the years are generous—and this book reflects their sharing nature. The tips and techniques featured here come from my own experience as an independent professional over the last 18 years, as well as from entrepreneurs around the country. When the call went out for frugal tips, suggestions came pouring in on postcards and in letters, as well as by fax and e-mail. (If you'd like to add your ideas for our next volume, check out the information in the back of the book on how to do so. It would be a pleasure to add your ideas to the next collection.)

This sense of community is one of the joys of entrepreneur-ship. As business owners, we understand that we're each engaged in unique endeavors, yet also share the same entrepreneurial challenges.

Frugal entrepreneurs, both new and seasoned, this book is a celebration of our kindred creative spirit. May you use it to build your business success!

Terri Lonier
New Paltz, NY

PUBLISHER'S NOTE

This book is designed to provide information in regard to the subject matter covered. It is sold with the understanding that the publisher and author are not engaged in rendering legal or financial advice. If legal or other expert assistance is required, the services of a competent professional should be sought.

While every effort has been made to make this book as complete and accurate as possible, information regarding small business and self-employment is constantly changing. Therefore, this book should be used as a general guide and with the understanding that it is not the ultimate source of small business information.

The purpose of this book is to educate and entertain. The author and Portico Press shall have neither liability nor responsibility to any person or entity with respect to any loss or damage caused, or alleged to be caused, directly or indirectly by the information contained in this book.

Any person not wishing to be bound by the above may return this book to the publisher for a refund.

Chapter 1

Office Operations

Success in any business springs from paying attention to the details of daily office operations. It's here where dreams meet reality, and plans get implemented. The tips in this chapter will provide you with insights into managing your office activities so that you can build a solid business foundation.

An Invisible Assistant

A well-designed office space is like an invisible assistant, helping you focus your energy and make best use of your time. The most efficient layouts tend to be in L-shaped or U-shaped configurations. Seated in the center of this "cockpit" in a swivel chair, you have easy access to frequently used files and equipment. Optimum layouts usually develop over time, as you refine your work style and habits. By staying aware of how well your office works as your partner, you can always be on the lookout for ways to improve its design. Of course, the flip side is that...

Immobility Can Be Painful

T he negative aspect of having all your work within arm's reach is that you easily can become much too sedentary. Over a period of time, this can have serious health consequences. Some entrepreneurs design their spaces so that they *must* get up once in a while. For example, they situate their printer, copier, or fax machine away from the desk (avoiding noxious odors and noisy incoming fax squeals), which forces them to get up and move now and again.

Expand Your Office

B e creative with unused "air" space on the walls and ceiling and under furniture. A tablecloth can create instant storage under any surface. Hanging things on walls or from the ceiling may stretch your office space many times over.

Thanks to Paulette Ensign

Paper First, Purchase Second

When you're ready to buy or build a new piece of office furniture, take time to plan it on paper first. Changes with pencil and eraser are much easier on mind and body than moving heavy equipment or bulky furniture. By assessing your work needs and available physical space first, you'll improve the odds that your investment will be worthwhile and can serve you for a long time.

Going, Going...Yours!

When it's time to outfit your workspace with furniture such as desks, chairs, computer stations, filing cabinets, or wall dividers, avoid the office furniture store. Instead, look in the newspaper for a business liquidation or auction. These are generally advertised on Saturdays and Sundays in the real estate or business sections of the paper. Businesses that are moving or closing often sell furniture at rock-bottom prices, which is a boon to frugal entrepreneurs.

Remember, even if you buy a brand-new desk, it will be *used* one day after you start working behind it. No one will ever refuse to sit at your desk because it isn't a new one. Save that money for business promotions or entertaining.

Thanks to Ron Hertenstein

Workstations

As much as your office space will allow, set up separate workstations for different activities, such as mailing, taking telephone orders, or quiet work time. Equip each station with appropriate supplies so activities can be completed efficiently. This approach helps you focus attention on specific tasks. It also gives a psychological boost by eliminating distractions and enabling you to complete work more quickly and easily.

Space Swap

If you're looking to move your business to another site (perhaps out of your home) and you're short on funds, consider bartering for space. Check out companies that may have some extra space and see if they would be willing to swap the space in exchange for a product or service your company can provide. It can be a win/win situation.

Temporary Excess

Another option is to check out companies in a growth mode. They often lease larger spaces, planning that they will fill them in the next few years. In the meantime, the space is unused, and the firms may be willing to sublease the space to you at a reduced rate. (Be sure to confirm the length of time you could stay.) As an interim solution, the short-term lease could be a frugal way to get quality office space for your growing business.

Gosh, I Hardly See You

A third space option harkens back to college days. Remember that roommate who fell madly in love and always spent time at their significant other's place instead of at yours? The same situation can transfer to the business world.

For example, some businesses maintain offices for sales representatives who spend most of their time on the road. Other firms establish tiny local offices away from main headquarters. Through networking in professional organizations and local business groups, you may find someone interested in sharing a space who travels quite frequently. You'd reap the benefits of splitting the costs yet having the space primarily for your own business.

Negotiate the Lease

L andlords will take tenants for term leases and some times require little to no rent money in the early months while you are starting out or trying to grow. To begin your search, look for office vacancy signs. Talk with owners of the properties, not leasing agents. Agents are paid a commission on the rent and are given guidelines by the owners of the properties. Cutting to the owner eliminates the middle person and often gives you more room to negotiate.

Thanks to Ron Hertenstein

Bulk Buying

Office supplies can be a lot cheaper when purchased in bulk quantities. Consider joining a warehouse club or creating your own buying group of like-minded frugal entrepreneurs. By pooling your purchases, you can enjoy bigger discounts and reduce your individual costs of mail-order shipping and handling fees. Some simple networking can bring you big savings.

Inventory Tally

Keep an inventory sheet of the office supplies you use in a handy spot, and update it on an ongoing basis. It's an easy way to track how much of a particular item you use, so you can take advantage of sales to stock up. An inventory record also helps you avoid the aggravation of interrupting your day to make a trip to the office-supply store because you've run out of a necessary item.

List in Hand

Most of us have experienced the phenomenon of shopping in a grocery store on an empty stomach with no list. Everything looks enticing, and our basket soon overflows with items we normally would not have purchased. The same is true of shopping in an office-supply superstore without a list. We're sure to walk out with things we don't need, only to forget the basics we came for. Walk in with a list, and you'll walk out with more money in your pocket.

Split the Storage

Do you have a dozen boxes of paper clips in your desk drawer? Desk space is too valuable to clutter up with excess supplies! Keep a small amount of regularly used supplies within arm's reach—near to where you'll be using them. Store excess inventory at a site removed from your immediate work area.

Annual Review

Set a time once a year to shop your main suppliers. Are they continuing to provide the best products or services? Are the prices competitive? Is the relationship worth continuing? Too often we become comfortable or complacent with our suppliers, accepting situations that are not in the best interest of our business. By establishing a specific time each year for supplier review, you can rectify any problems, negotiate for better pricing, strengthen the relationship, or find another source.

Ship It!

Once you add up the time, the gasoline, the wear and tear on your car *and* on you, you'll begin to rethink the value of buying by mail. Before you leave your office, check to see if you can order your desired item by phone. Businesses spend billions of dollars ordering from catalogs each year, and there's a reason. Let UPS and FedEx do your carting. It's good business sense.

Personal Shorthand

Create your own shorthand system for taking notes during meetings or on the telephone. For example, phrases such as "Left message, call back" can translate to "lm/cb." Other commonly used titles or phrases related to your specific business can often be represented by a few initials. Be creative in developing your own private language, and save yourself time and energy—as well as ink and paper!

In Good Form

If you find yourself writing the same information over and over again, design a form to handle the task. Similarly, you can create templates for basic letters and other documents you generate on your computer. With essential formatting already in place, you'll save time, energy, and paper since you won't have to check your work and rewrite drafts. Pop in the date, inside address, and other personalized information, and your letter is ready to print.

Think Retrieval

When creating a file for something, name it by the first thing that comes to your mind when you ask yourself, "What word will I think of first when I go to look for this again?" instead of "Where should I put this?" The only "right" place to put a file is where you'll be able to locate it again when you need it.

Thanks to Barbara Hemphill

Fewer Places to Look... and Lose!

Most filing systems have too many files. It is easier to go through one file with 20 pieces of paper than 10 files with two papers in each. It's better to put information into the largest general category first. Then, if that file becomes too bulky, break it down. In rare instances, an important document may merit a separate file if there is no existing file in which it could be easily found.

Thanks to Barbara Hemphill

Win the War

Successful entrepreneurs understand that an enemy invades their office every day in the form of a glut of mail. If you don't attack it on a daily basis, it soon accumulates and takes over every available surface. Make a habit of sorting daily mail by standing over a wastebasket and recycling bin. Discard any materials—such as outer envelopes of bills—that you know you'll toss later. Make a preliminary sort of letters, invoices, and oversized items such as catalogs. Then tackle each pile to completion. With a system and a sense of determination, your daily mail can be conquered.

The Art of Wastebasketry

It is no longer practical—or perhaps even possible—to keep all the information that arrives in your office. When determining what to keep or to toss, ask yourself these questions: Does this information require any action on my part? Does this information exist elsewhere? Is this information recent enough to be useful? Can I identify the specific circumstances when I would use this information? Are there any tax or legal implications?

The key question, however, is: What is the worst possible thing that could happen if I did not have this information? If you are willing to live with the results, toss it. If not, keep it.

Resource: Kiplinger's Taming the Office Tiger *by Barbara Hemphill (Times Business Books)*

Manila or Hanging?

When deciding between manila file folders or hanging file folders, think about how you will access the information they contain. If you will be removing the file folder from the drawer frequently, opt for a hanging file folder to support the interior manila one.

In contrast, if there are only a few sheets of paper that you refer to infrequently, keep them loose in a hanging file. It will take up less space and save you the cost of additional manila file folders. For older files accessed infrequently or placed in storage, consider eliminating the hanging file folders altogether.

Friendly Reminder

Put all papers that need your response—such as bills, invitations, or notes—into a tickler file that gets opened on a daily basis. This will serve as a reminder that these items need attention, and will keep you on track.

Thanks to Sheila Delson

Color Coding

When setting up your filing system, consider investing in colored file folders. While they may be a bit more expensive, color-coded files can save you valuable time when searching for documents. Think about establishing different colors for types of files— such as green for financial matters, red for "hot" projects, blue for suppliers, or yellow for specific projects. With a color-based system, you'll be able to determine the general type of information inside the file even from across a room.

Changeover in Process

When introducing a new filing system (such as color) into your office operations, merge it slowly. For example, decide that all *new* files will be done in a certain way, or that files in a specific drawer or section will be changing over. This will be less disruptive than changing all your files at once, and you'll be more likely to start the process instead of waiting for a free moment when you can redo hundreds of files.

Clutter Liberation

Is your office filled with clutter that you just can't seem to toss out? You keep telling yourself, "Someday...."

Here's a motivational insight: If the stuff is going to end up at the dump or recycling center someday, what's going to increase its value between now and then? The only thing it's doing is causing you guilt or a knot in your stomach each time you see it. It's going to be tossed sooner or later. Why not make it sooner? The sense of freedom is a sweet reward.

Thanks to Sheila Delson

Chapter 2

Technology

Technology is the frugal entrepreneur's most powerful tool. It streamlines complex tasks and enables us to do many things at once. It also dissolves distance and makes our world smaller by allowing us to share news and information easily. These tips remind us to use technology with care, so we don't focus only on the tool and lose sight of our ultimate goal.

Capture Those Ideas

Successful entrepreneurs know the impact a single good idea can have on a business. Realizing that inspiration can strike at any time, they make sure they capture those brainstorms. Consider keeping a microcassette recorder handy to make verbal notes throughout the day. (Some nonstop thinkers even keep a unit next to their bed to record middle-of-the-night insights.) If you spend much time in your car, keep a recorder in the glove compartment, or a pen and notepad close at hand.

Thanks to Christine Puliselic

Teach It by Tape

Need to give a lengthy explanation for a project and don't want to write several pages of instructions? Consider recording your instructions on tape. It's likely to be a quicker solution, and your words can be played back several times for clarity.

Recorded Correspondence

Taped messages are also a great way to stay in touch with busy colleagues. You can record your thoughts over the space of a day, then send them off for less than the cost of a lengthy phone call. Your colleagues can listen to your news while driving in their car or working out at the gym, then respond by recording on the other side of the tape. An added bonus: The warmth of your voice and personality can shine through.

Use Your Head(set)

If you think that telephone headsets are only for secretaries or telemarketers, you're missing out on a great productivity tool. Studies show that using a headset can improve your productivity up to 43%. With both hands free, you can be a whiz at doing multiple activities while on the phone, including typing or pulling files buried deep in cabinet drawers. You'll also be doing your body a favor, since you won't be crunching your neck into uncomfortable poses. The newest models feature cordless units, so you can roam up to 50 feet from your desk with no wires to restrict you.

Resource: *Hello Direct, (800) 444-3556 or via the Internet at http://www.hello-direct.com*

Toll-Free Competition

One of the hallmarks of big business used to be the availability of a toll-free number for information or ordering. Now even the smallest of businesses can be immediately on par with their biggest competitors. With the proliferation of long-distance resellers, toll-free numbers (both the 800 and new 888 exchanges) are available at rates averaging only a few pennies a minute. Services can also be established for certain states or areas, depending on your customer base and needs.

Resource: *Paulin Communications, (800) 324-9449*

Piggyback a Telephone Line

Before you install expensive telephone wiring, consider subscribing to a "distinctive ringing" service from your local telephone company. For only a few dollars a month, this option allows you to establish an independent telephone number that piggybacks on existing wiring. The new number has a different ringing pattern to indicate which telephone number the incoming caller is using. It lets you decide in advance which greeting to use to answer the call, and it's a great way to train family members to answer a home-based business line in a professional manner.

Thanks to Kenneth Koubek and Maria Pearson

Separate but Equal

There's no reason that home-based businesses need to have more than one business-rate telephone line. A business line provides directory listings and visibility for your business, but basic service and outgoing local calls generally are billed at much higher rates. Instead, have additional residential lines installed for fax machines, modems, and supplemental voice lines. Target the business line primarily for incoming calls, and use the cheaper residential lines for everything else.

Changeover Instead of Install

Many entrepreneurs set up a home-based business and decide they want to establish a business telephone line so they can be listed in the Yellow Pages and other business directories. The shock hits when they discover that the installation charges for a business line can be several hundred dollars.

Frugal entrepreneurs know that it costs much less to change a residential line to a business line, since the wiring is already in place. Be kind to your budget: when setting up or expanding your home-based business, install an additional residential line first. A few months later, call the phone company to change one of the lines over to an "official" business line. You'll find that the changeover fee is substantially less than new business line installation charges.

Speedy Message Retrieval

Tired of punching in all those numbers to retrieve your voice mail? Program your speed dialer with those frequently used access numbers. You'll be hitting only two or three buttons instead of more than a dozen—and over the course of a business week, you'll save yourself loads of time. For security reasons, take care when programming your personal identification number into your phone, or else others may have access to private messages.

Retrieval on the Road

Calling in for voice mail messages while on the road can be an arduous task of dialing in sequences of dozens of credit card numbers and access codes. Make one slip, and you're forced to start over. Busy travelers invest in a small digital device that is programmed to hold your personal access codes and frequently dialed numbers. Holding the device next to the telephone's mouthpiece creates the digital tones needed to complete the call, eliminating nearly all of the dialing. Your fingers will thank you.

Resources: *Radio Shack stores nationwide*

Paulin Communications, (800) 324-9449

Paging to the Max

Pagers can be great, but it's often frustrating when you want to leave a detailed message, or when you know you won't be at a phone where the recipient can return your call. Instead, call the person's voice mail and leave a full message, along with options for next-step actions. Then call the person's pager, and instead of entering *your* telephone number, punch in their own voice mail number. That way, they'll be directed to call their voice mail (often a local call for them), where they'll hear your recorded message with all the details.

Thanks to Ed Dudkowski

Digital Note-Taker

If you get a brainstorm while you're away from the office, here's an inexpensive way to make sure you don't let it slip away: call your voice mail or answering machine and leave yourself a message. The technology is always ready to record those inspirations—even those middle-of-the-night insights. Once the information is captured, your mind will be free to focus on more important matters.

Internet Access

Eager to get an online connection to the Internet and want to avoid commercial rates? Check with a local school or university. If you're a member of the faculty or staff, your account may be underwritten by the school. Or you may decide to take a class and qualify for a student account. Either way, the university rates are likely to be much lower than commercial ones.

Thanks to Kim Mosley

Laptop Viewing

It's ten minutes before your slide presentation, and suddenly you want to make some changes to your talk. With a light box for slide sorting nowhere to be found, you pull out your laptop computer and set the screen's brightness control to "high." Voilà! An instant backlit surface for sorting your slides.

Recycled Disks

If you're on any computer-related mailing list, chances are high that you've received several copies of free demo software from online services. Instead of tossing the extra disks, reformat the floppies and use them for extra backups, transferring data between machines, or sending files to friends through the mail. The quality of the disks is pretty good, since the manufacturers don't want to risk customers having trouble trying out their product. Recycling the disks for your own use is a way to be kind to the earth and be a frugal techno-entrepreneur as well.

Label Wires Before Moving

Before you disassemble any configuration of your computer or office technology, take time to label the wires. Simple file folder labels, wrapped around the wiring, will do the trick. Using a pen or marker, clearly indicate what the wire connects—if necessary, with a label at each end.

If it's a complex system, consider using color-coded labels or markers, and draw a diagram of the system's wiring. This approach can save you hours of time and eliminate the frustration of staring at a tangled pile of gray wires that are the key to your system getting up and running again.

Technology Birds of a Feather

If you haven't joined a computer user group yet, you're missing out on one of the most valuable technology resources around. These organizations, which range in size from a group of a dozen people to associations of more than 10,000 members, are designed to help individuals get the most out of their computing experience. Groups exist for every type of computer and software, literally all over the world. Computer enthusiasts gather on a regular basis—usually once a month—and share news, information, and tips on technology. (They don't share commercial software, because copying software that's not shareware or freeware is illegal.)

For example, you can get feedback on equipment you're considering, or hints on how to tackle new tasks with your software. User group meetings are a great way to network with other entrepreneurs, and to find gurus who can lead you through the maze of complex technology decisions.

To connect with a user group near you, contact your local computer retailer and ask about upcoming meetings. Many groups also run announcements in local newspapers or computer publications.

Resources: *User Group Connection, (408) 461-5700 or on the Internet at http://www.ugconnection.com*

User Group Network, on the Internet at http://www.user-groups.com

Freeware and Shareware

One of the benefits of subscribing to an online service or a user group is the ability to get freeware and shareware. Written by computer programmers with a generous spirit, these applications usually are designed for specific tasks, such as generating labels, keeping track of hourly billing, or organizing files. Other freeware includes graphics, illustrations, or public-domain logos such as the recycling symbol.

Freeware, as the name implies, is for distribution without charge. Shareware comes with the name and address of the programmer, who requests that if you try the program and decide to keep it, you send a small fee (usually $5–30) as payment.

A creative twist to this approach is postcardware, which requests "payment" of an interesting postcard sent to the programmer in exchange for the application. These inexpensive but valuable programs can be downloaded from online computer forums or obtained from user groups who sell them on floppy disks or as huge collections on a CD-ROM.

Faxing in the Wee Hours

To save money on fax charges—particularly those sent internationally—see if your fax machine can be programmed to make calls at specific times. If so, your machine can initiate the fax during evening or late-night hours, when rates are lower.

On Time, On Track

Find an "integrated" personal information manager (PIM) to track your calendar, contacts, and To-Do list. The integration allows you to transfer information easily within one program. For example, if you have a meeting with someone, the program will automatically link the individual's address and telephone number with the record. It may save only a few seconds, but over a few weeks or months, those moments add up!

Software "Boom Boxes"

Uncertain about what piece of software to buy first for your new computer? Check out the products that say "works" in their name (for example, ClarisWorks or Microsoft Works). These programs integrate functions of word processing, outlining, database, spreadsheet, graphics, presentations, charting, and communications in a single package.

The all-in-one design is similar in concept to a music boom box: you get a range of capabilities at a reasonable price (the software runs about $125 or so). If you're interested in a top-of-the-line individual component, you can always invest in it later. For most general computing uses, and particularly for newcomers, the "boom box" approach to software is an economical and efficient solution.

Bundle Bonuses

When buying a piece of technology, always find out if any products come bundled with the purchase. Technology companies are fiercely competitive marketers, and they'll often give away free copies of software as a premium when you buy a strategic partner's product. By shopping around and asking for bundle deals, you can increase the overall value of your purchase.

Upgrades and Sidegrades

Buying software is similar to subscribing to a magazine. To get the "latest and greatest" features, the companies will entice you to buy the upgrades to their products. Once you register your software, you are eligible to buy the newest version (as an upgrade) for about half to a third of the cost to a first-time buyer. The companies figure, and rightly so, that the investment you have spent in time and energy in learning their product will keep you a loyal customer.

To break this cycle, competitors often offer *sidegrades*. These deals enable you to buy the full version of their software at the discounted upgrade price if you can prove that you're a registered user of their competitor's product. Frugal entrepreneurs register their software to take advantage of upgrades, and keep their eyes open for sidegrade offers of competitive products if they're thinking of switching software.

Gently Used

If you don't mind owning a piece of office equipment that's been gently used, check out companies that offer remanufactured models. The systems are often demo models, overstock, out-of-date units, or returns, and the companies cannot legally sell them as new. Most such equipment comes with a warranty, although it is generally shorter than one that comes with new products. To take best advantage of remanufactured equipment, it helps to be up to speed on model numbers and features. That way, you can be sure you're investing in equipment that will serve you best.

Thanks to Lucy Mundo

Used Copiers Can Be Powerful

For the same money you'd spend on a low-cost "personal" copier, you can get a used high-end office copier with loads of great features. Dealers will often have copiers that have come off lease, been returned due to lease default, or simply been used for a trade-in. Extended warranty options can bring you peace of mind, and in some cases there may even be a buy-back option.

Thanks to Allison Kozak and Ron Hertenstein

Used Phone Systems, Too

Contact the local sellers of telephone systems that are not related to the telephone company and ask them about used systems. They often will have removed a system from a business that did not need it, or the company traded it in for a newer one. The used system will have most of the bells and whistles for a fraction of the cost of a new one. The savings is yours!

Thanks to Ron Hertenstein

Scan, Don't Type

When you're faced with a project requiring extensive retyping of photocopied or faxed material, consider using scanners and OCR (optical character recognition) software. The combination of these two technologies can save you countless hours of keyboarding.

Thanks to Allison Kozak

Zap Curling Paper

If your office environment is very humid, you may be having problems with paper curling in your laser printer or photocopier, particularly if you're printing double-sided sheets. The culprit is the moisture in the paper. Try placing the opened package in your microwave oven for about a minute and a half on the high setting. The moisture is pulled off as steam, and your printing will go smoothly.

Thanks to Mark McBride and Publishing and Production Executive *magazine*

Less Dense, More Value

Be good to the environment and your pocketbook by lowering the density on your photocopier and computer printer when making everyday copies and printouts. Your cartridges will last longer, and so will your office-supply budget.

Thanks to Sheila Zia

Folders as a Directory

Sometimes launching a database for telephone numbers you access on a regular basis is just overkill. A simple solution is to create a master folder filled with empty folders. The titles of the empty folders are the abbreviated names and telephone numbers (or extensions) you call on a regular basis. Keep this master folder on your computer desktop within easy access, and it can save you lots of time.

Thanks to Neil Trager

Crack the Manuals

Even though computer and office-equipment manuals seem to be written in a foreign language, you can save time and energy in the long run by taking time to read them. It's also worthwhile to use the tutorials that come with new software. They are carefully designed to lead you through the features of the program, often by having you create sample projects. It's one of the best ways to boost your productivity with a new technology tool.

Total Costs Add Up

When choosing a piece of office technology, be sure you calculate *all* the costs of owning it. Don't forget to factor supplies, maintenance, and repair costs into your comparisons. Also consider the ease and cost of finding the supplies or repair personnel. The unit may have the lowest purchase price, but it may not be the best value for your business in the long run.

Chapter 3

Marketing

Marketing is an area in which frugal entrepreneurs can allow their creativity to really shine. Nothing is off limits if it succeeds in connecting your business with new and regular customers. Let these tips inspire you to expand your ideas about marketing your business. Once you've adopted the frugal marketing mindset, the options are endless.

Clarity Is Power

Do you know what business you're in—and can you explain it in one sentence? Fuzzy thinking can lead to lots of wasted time, energy, and money in marketing your business. Take the time to clearly identify what your business is and what customers you serve. Once focused, your efforts are like a laser beam, guiding you in every decision and helping you hit your target goals more easily.

Marketing Mindset

Savvy entrepreneurs understand that one of the most powerful marketing tools costs nothing at all: it's your attitude. When you think of *every aspect* of your business in terms of its marketing impact, then even simple things take on new importance. This ranges from the design of your letterhead to the way you introduce yourself. Give yourself a mental checkup and see how fine-tuned your marketing mindset is.

Six Magic Words

The six most important words you can say to your customers are: "How did you hear about us?" Their answers will guide you in determining how effective your marketing has been, and where you should invest your future marketing dollars.

Become a Guerrilla!

Guerrillas are fiercely independent fighters who are committed to a cause and use every possible method and tool to win. If you think that sounds a lot like an entrepreneur, you've captured the idea of guerrilla marketing.

Guerrilla entrepreneurs climb into their customer's head and focus all their marketing from the *buyer's* perspective. They build relationships with individuals, knowing that people would rather buy from someone they know.

Think about what you can do to establish a personal connection with your customers. Then repeat the contact with them on a regular, ongoing basis. Guerrillas know that time is their ally, and that most businesses give up too soon. Capturing valuable repeat customers who bring long-term success is the ultimate victory.

Resources: Guerrilla Marketing *and the* Guerrilla Marketing *book series by Jay Conrad Levinson (Houghton Mifflin)*

Guerrilla Marketing Newsletter, *see Resources, page 147*

Guerrilla Marketing Online, on the Internet at http://www.gmarketing.com

Go with Those You Know

Knowing your competition and targeting businesses that already are familiar with you will enable you to focus your marketing efforts to highlight your strengths. It will also help get your marketing materials in the hands of true decision-makers, avoiding the frustration of having them passed around like "hot potatoes."

Thanks to Jason Brand

Ideal Customers

Create a strong mental picture of the ideal customers for your business. Imagine the type of people they are in terms of demographic profile, such as gender, education, income, and family. Then push the limits and think of them as individuals, and of what their personal characteristics are—for example, his or her favorite movie, or type of food, or recreational activity. Jump into their minds and think about what they need—and how your business can answer that desire. Customers are not a nebulous population, "out there." Thinking of them as individuals will lead you to a better understanding of how to market your products and services.

Where's the Pain?

Customers buy your product or service because it solves a problem for them. The fact that your widget comes in 12 colors or 7 speeds matters less to them than the fact that it can save them time, money, or aggravation. Always strive to communicate the *benefits* of your product or service, not merely the *features*. Ask yourself, "Where's their pain?" The answer will guide you in addressing your customers' real needs, and will keep your business focused on providing valuable benefits to them.

Thanks to Dan Poynter

Referrals and Testimonials

Word-of-mouth continues to be one of the best marketing methods, since personal comments about your business carry with them the credibility of the person saying them.

The best testimonials tell a story, in capsule form: the problem the client brought to you, the solution you provided, and how things are different for the client now that your solution has worked its magic. Alternatively, the story could be: the client was in search of a special experience (like a wonderful vacation or new hairstyle), the client came to you, and now their life is more wonderful for it!

Resources: Referral Magic: 17 Ways to Let Your Clients Do Your Selling *(72-minute audio, $29.95)* and How to Write Letters That Make Your Phone Ring *(45-minute audio, $19.95) by David Garfinkel, (415) 564-4475*

Get It in Writing

When a client raves to you about how great their experience has been with your business, take notes on their specific feedback. At the end of the conversation, summarize what they've said and ask them if they'd be willing to put these comments in writing. Most will gladly say yes. When dealing with busy individuals, offer to draft a letter based on their verbal testimonial and fax it to them for editing and final output on their letterhead. By taking the initiative, you make it easy for individuals to complete these testimonial letters. It's an effective way to build a powerful marketing portfolio.

Thanks to Judy Byers

Opening the Door

Take one of your best clients out to dinner and ask them if they would support you in your introduction to their client list, in return for a commission or a reciprocal business favor. The endorsement could come in the form of a letter of recommendation, written by you with their approval. Ask what kind of service they would appreciate in return.

Thanks to Victoria Chorbajian

Write a Winning Bio

Take time to write several biographical summaries of yourself and your business. Make one short (a few paragraphs) and one longer (up to two pages). Before you begin, think about the end results you want to create for the intended receiver. Then include credentials that prove you have achieved similar results for other businesses with whom your prospects can identify. If you have several distinct groups of prospects, you may want to write several bios, each tailored to a specific need or audience.

Frugal entrepreneurs know that a bio can be a powerful marketing tool, since it gives you the power to determine precisely how you want to be presented. Well-crafted bios are often reprinted with little or no editing.

Thanks to David Garfinkel

Charity Is Good for Business

Attend charity events and fundraisers and circulate, circulate, circulate. The people you meet may lead you to your next business contract—and your ticket may even be tax deductible. Consider bidding on auctioned-for-charity items that could also qualify as business entertainment deductions or business gifts, such as theater tickets or dinner packages.

Thanks to Mary Beth Gehl

Marketing by Voice Mail

Voice mail can do more than just capture incoming messages. Make the most of your outgoing voice mail announcement by including in it a brief "sound bite" of marketing news. For example, you can mention a new product or service, or a recent award. It's a great way to bring customers up to date on news of your company, and can be a great conversation starter when you call them back. Just remember to keep it to a few seconds, and weave it into your general announcement.

Faxes with a Bonus

Don't let that cover sheet of yours slip through that fax machine with all that white space! Make sure it carries a short blurb about your company, a new announcement, special sale, or other tidbit. You're reaching a captive customer, so make every contact work for you.

Labels Prevent Orphans

When promoting your business, be sure that your company's name, address, and telephone number appear on every item you send out. This is particularly important when sending out packets ofinformation that may get torn apart and routed to separate departments.

A cover letter with complete contact information may get tossed, leaving the heart of your package with no mention of your firm. Review your materials as if they might end up as "orphaned" elements. Would they carry your message well?

Marketing Partners

Expand your marketing reach by networking with business owners who offer complementary, but not competing, products or services. Consider creative ways to piggyback on each other's client base: circulating each other's marketing materials, packaging bundles of products or services, offering discounts to mutual clients, sharing advertising costs, or splitting trade show expenses. These alliances can raise the visibility of each individual business, creating a marketing impact much greater than any single business can attain alone.

Your 60-Second Brag

When you're introduced, the first words out of your mouth can send a powerful marketing message about you and your company. Unfortunately, these phrases are second nature to most people, and they're often filled with self-deprecating comments.

Take time to develop a "60-Second Brag" about yourself and your business. It's not meant to turn you into an egotistical bore. Instead, it's designed to give you the self-confidence to speak spontaneously about yourself for several minutes.

Begin by listing all the things you'd like someone to know about you and your company. Then practice turning those ideas into interesting conversation phrases. You'll find yourself adapting your "brag" to different social and business settings. You'll also refine your comments, based on the feedback and responses you get. Armed with a well-prepared "60-Second Brag," you can turn any spontaneous encounter into a big win for you and your business.

Express Elevator Version

A cousin to the "60-Second Brag" is the briefer version you use when you have only a few moments to engage someone in conversation—say, on an elevator. With practice, you can capture the essence of your business in a short "sound bite." Think of it as a *verbal* business card. Like the traditional paper ones, when it is designed well, it can have a lasting impact on potential clients and customers.

Newsletters

Newsletters are a great way to build an ongoing relationship with your customers. Frugal entrepreneurs devise creative ways to make their newsletters memorable without breaking their budget. Consider options such as a single, folded sheet with name and address information merge-printed from a laser printer (no labels or envelopes to worry about). Other inventive marketers have designed postcard-sized newsletters. They're colorful and cheaper to mail—and they're often saved on bulletin boards or refrigerators.

Resource: *Newsletter Resources, (314) 647-0400; free catalog with a self-addressed stamped envelope*

Who's Got the Button?

Buttons and pins are a common promotional item, but often require minimum orders of a thousand for manufacture. You can make limited-edition, inexpensive buttons by taking images from a color laser printer or photocopier to your local copy shop for lamination. Trim the excess, tape on a jewelry pin back (found at a local craft-supply store), and presto!—a ready-to-wear mini-billboard for your lapel.

It's Who You Know

L eads clubs are groups of individuals who support each other's sales efforts and share leads and contacts. Some are formal organizations, while others are casual gatherings. The concept is similar: only one person per industry or type of business can join, thereby eliminating any conflicts of competing for the same customer. Whether you join a more structured group or create your own informal network, sharing leads is one of the best frugal ways to leverage your business efforts.

Resource: *Ali Lassen's Leads Club, (800) 783-3761*

Business Card Display

D o you ever get frustrated carrying business cards and one of those little display holders for them? The cards don't always stay safe, and the little holder often doesn't fit anywhere easily. Here's a creative solution: Take a hard cassette box (often called a Norelco case) and open it. Break off the two little projections that are meant to immobilize the tape reels. You now have a box that's just the right size for carrying business cards. Better yet, the box opens up to make a nifty tabletop display stand for your cards when you need it.

Thanks to Odette Pollar and Wally Bock

Double Duty

When exhibiting at trade shows, use a white board with an easel for a background on which to display your products or as a way to announce show specials. After the show, the board can be used in your office, or on presentations for outlining transactions.

Thanks to Ron Hertenstein

Maximize Your Trade Show

Trade shows are an excellent source of sales opportunities, but not every show is right for your business. The most important factor for success is having a clear idea of what you'd like the show to accomplish for your company. Build awareness? Introduce new products? Sign up new accounts? With answers to such questions in hand, you can better determine which show would be a good match.

Be sure to attend a few shows before you decide to exhibit. See what your competition is doing, and decide how you will present your firm. With proper planning, a show can be a worthwhile investment instead of a big expense.

Resource: 49 Ways to Be Your Best at Trade Show Selling, *booklet by Mark S. A. Smith, $3.70, from The Valence Group, (800) 745-4549*

Strategize Your Attack

When visiting a trade show, it's easy to become overwhelmed at the number of booths and information available to you. To get the most out of the show, spend the first half hour in a quiet spot with the show guide and booth floor plan. This will give you an overview of the show and enable you to create a strategy for maximizing your visit.

You might want to bring some colored markers along to highlight booths you don't want to miss. With annotated map in hand, you can relax and enjoy the show, knowing you have already chosen what is most important for you to see.

Free Can Be Expensive

Before you're so quick to pick up all that free trade show literature, consider if it is really worthwhile to you. Too often, we end up carting the stuff around, only to bring it home and have it accumulate in piles on the floor or in some back file drawer. While we didn't pay money for it, it did cost us in energy to carry it home and later send it off to the recycling center. Save your back, save the planet. Think before you take that free literature.

Second Suitcase

Seasoned conference and trade show attendees know this trick: take along a second, collapsible suitcase that tucks inside your primary bag on the outbound trip. The spare will conveniently hold all the materials you pick up along the way.

Thanks to Rebecca Morgan

Ship the Catalogs—or the Sweaters!

If you don't carry your trade show literature home, consider shipping it direct to your office from the trade show site. Many events now offer this service. Or, consider freeing some luggage space by shipping home your lighter and bulkier clothing (cheaper than heavy catalogs and other papers).

Chapter 4

Printing

Printing expenses can devour an entrepreneur's budget in the wink of an eye. This chapter presents some creatively frugal ways to get the most out of putting ink on paper. Whether your goal is a simple one-color business card or a fancy full-color catalog, these ideas can help stretch your printing dollars and give you a bigger return on your investment.

Postcard Power

Postcards are a terrific frugal marketing tool. They're colorful, they're less expensive to print and mail than letters, and they can capture a potential customer's attention quickly. Best of all, instead of automatically hitting the trash when your message arrives, your postcard may end up saved on a bulletin board or refrigerator.

Resource: *Carl Sebastian Colour printing company, (800) 825-0381*

Recycled Scratch Pads

Before you toss old flyers, forms, or letterhead, take them to your local "quick print" firm and see if you can turn the outdated excess into scratch pads. Sheets can be trimmed to nearly any size, and inexpensively edged with adhesive "padding" so they can become tear-off pads. With a little luck, old letterhead can be trimmed to eliminate the obsolete address and phone number, leaving sheets with only your company name on them—a perfect solution for informal notes.

Postcard-Sized Labels

Many laser printers can print postcards. Sometimes, however, it means hand feeding them or fussing with special setups. A time-saving option is to print your message on a large laser label (such as Avery 5164) and attach the labels to the cards. Since the labels come six to a sheet, your printing time can be reduced significantly. You can also save the labels and adhere them to other marketing pieces, such as pocket folders or envelopes.

Resource: *Avery Laser Printer labels, available in all sizes*

Design Experience Pays Off

By working with an experienced graphic designer or printer, you can create the impact of an expensive piece on a budget. Design professionals can incorporate tricks and techniques they've picked up over the years. The fees you invest in experienced talent can save you time, energy, and money in the long run.

Two for the Price of One

Through the creative use of tints and screens in the printing process, you can often create the impression of multiple colors from only two or three ink colors. A single color, such as navy, can be run dark to carry type and photos, and screened to create light blue background boxes or graphics.

Similarly, two ink colors can be blended to create the look of three or more. Keep in mind that some colors create tints more effectively than others. (For example, red may be powerful, but a tint of light pink may not communicate your message well.)

Gang Printing

The greatest expense of any printing project is getting the press rolling. Frugal entrepreneurs can save money by shopping around to locate printers who do "gang" printing. These printers will combine jobs (such as printing postcards or brochures) and print the work of several clients at once. The economies of scale are then shared by each of the clients. This approach works best if you have a flexible time schedule and your printed piece doesn't require any special preparation, ink colors, or trimming.

No-Scrap Printing

The next time you're designing a project to be printed, be sure to determine if you'll have any extra space on the sheet of paper. (Paper used on printing presses comes in standard large-sheet sizes, and the excess is usually trimmed off and discarded as scrap.) Frugal entrepreneurs maximize their printing dollar by including small projects such as bookmarks, cards, or coupons on the main sheet. This tactic means the only charge will be trimming, with the paper and printing of the extra projects essentially free!

Paper as Another Color

Instead of opting for a simple white sheet for your next business card or brochure, explore the possibilities of using colored paper. Color and texture add visual interest, and give the impression of a classier piece—often for just a few pennies more. A distinctive paper can raise your message above the reams of basic black-ink-on-white-paper that deluge our mailboxes every day.

Savings by the Ounce

Remember that your choice of paper for a printed project can also have a significant impact on your postage costs. For example, slight differences in the weight of paper for an 8-page newsletter can mean a single issue is mailed at either the 1-ounce rate or the almost double 2-ounce rate.

Before you print, make a mockup of your piece from sample paper stock and weigh it carefully. Be sure to calculate the extra weight of cover envelopes, stickers, or labels, too.

Stationery by Mail

If your stationery needs are fairly straightforward, you might be able to save money by purchasing items such as business cards, letterhead, envelopes, or Rolodex cards by mail. Printers often specialize in certain items, so be sure to ask for a sample kit and a price list of their line.

Thanks to Tom Antion

Resource: *Pro Litho, (413) 532-9473*

The Single-Sheet Solution

By analyzing how your business uses paper, you can multiply the impact of your printing budget. Think about what kinds of sheets you use, in what quantities, and how they may be similar. Plan your future paper usage based on the past, and plan printing to meet the anticipated demand. Once you know what you need, it's a simple process of ganging printing jobs onto a single sheet. For instance, your newsletter shells could also be fact sheets or product catalog sheets. Your letterhead could be a version of your newsletter. Your invoices could be your letterhead.

One business used this approach to get letterhead, fact sheets, monthly calendars, monthly newsletters, and reply notes all out of a single sheet. They were all printed at the same time, on the same press, using the same ink colors. After the larger sheets were trimmed, the company used laser printers and duplicators to individualize the pieces as needed.

There are dozens of ways to configure this strategy to your needs. Another common approach is with cover stock for your "hard paper" needs, such as business cards, table tents, brochures, or small posters. With a little preplanning, you can reap considerable savings in your printing costs and stretch your printing budget.

Resource: The Single Sheet Solution *by Fred Showker, part of the PowerHouse Publishing collection of disk-based tutorials and electronic template files on graphic design topics; details available by e-mail at showker@graphic-design.com or via the Internet at http://www.graphic-design.com*

Partners for Economy

When it's time to get a project printed, involve your printer from the early stages. They know their equipment and capabilities, and can often suggest ways to economize. At the start of the project, make a dummy to show things such as folds, screens, or colors. Building your design around the printer's capabilities will give you a better finished product.

Resource: *101 Ways to Save Money on Newsletters by Polly Pattison, $7.95, from Newsletter Resources, (314) 647-0400*

Preprinted Masters

If you're doing an ongoing series of printed pieces, such as a newsletter or a collection of special reports, you can save money and create two-color impact by having the second color printed on the full quantity of paper stock right from the start. For example, banners, boxes, or ruled lines can all be printed in color. When each issue is ready to go, you select a portion of the preprinted stock and print the main copy (usually in black).

The trick is to accurately estimate your needs for the entire project. Many printers will store the full supply of preprinted stock, knowing they are securing your business for the duration of the project.

Consolidate and Save

If you find a printing company that serves you well, let them know you are considering consolidating all your printing work with them. With this leverage you can often negotiate better pricing, payment terms, and customer service.

Tuesday Is Brown

It's expensive to wash up presses, so some quick printers have a certain day of the week for each color. Decide what color you want and find out the day it's offered.

Resource: 101 Ways to Save Money on Newsletters *by Polly Pattison, $7.95, from Newsletter Resources, (314) 647-0400*

Chapter 5

Direct Mail

Successful direct mail marketing is a masterful blend of art and science. The crafting of a creative message must be matched with the discipline of proper list usage and tracking. When art and science converge, the results can be remarkable—and rewarding. The tips in this chapter are designed to help you maximize your marketing efforts and bring profits to your mailbox.

Your List Is Golden

Aside from financial records, there is nothing more valuable to your business than your customer mailing list. Successful entrepreneurs know who their customers are and stay in contact with them on a regular basis. Treat your mailing list like gold—because it really *is* like money in the bank. Keep it updated on a regular basis, and store copies of it in a secure place away from your office, such as your safe deposit box at the bank.

List Cleaning

If you do a lot of bulk mailing, it's important to keep your mailing list clean, since mail is not forwarded. If your list is stored on computer, a mailing service bureau can correct the addresses electronically by cross-checking them with national database directories. The cost of their updates is worth the savings in your postage and in materials not heading toward the dumpster.

Free Cleaning

If you have a large database in computerized format, the United States Postal Service (USPS) offers a one-time cleaning and ZIP code check. This complimentary disk conversion service cross-checks your PC-compatible files with the USPS national database of addresses. You'll receive full ZIP+4 address information, and notes on what may be wrong or missing with your addresses. Cleaner addresses and ZIP+4 means postal savings. Ask your local post office for the phone number of the postal business center serving your area.

Mailing Service = Multiple Benefits

A good relationship with a mailing service can be invaluable to budget-minded entrepreneurs doing large mailings. Since your direct mail will go out under their postal permit, you eliminate the need and expense of paying permit fees on your own. You can use their printed indicia instead of stamps, which saves you time. Because they're doing the sorting and mailing, you enjoy lower rates. You also don't need to learn complex postal regulations. For these reasons and more, it's a smart choice to use a mailing service. The fees they charge are well worth the savings in time, energy, and money.

Thanks to Edward D. Lekson

Avoiding the Morgue

If you haven't cleaned your mailing list in a while, you can be sure that a certain percentage of your customers have moved. To prevent your direct mail from ending up in the dead letter office, add the line "or current resident" to your address label. That way, the letter will be delivered to the address, even if your intended recipient has moved. Your marketing message may not generate a new customer, but at least your chances are better than zero—which is what they would have been in the post office trash.

Thanks to Nancy Stanich and Dorrit Berg

Telegraph Your Message

When designing your direct mail piece, keep head lines short. Think in terms of billboard messages. You only have only a few seconds to grab a reader's attention. A good rule of thumb is to use 11 words or less.

Thanks to Markus Allen

Resource: *Mail Advertising Hotline (weekly updates), (601) 325-7899*

Track Your Efforts

Whenever you create a direct mail piece or ad, be sure to set up a system to track what lists worked best. One of the easiest ways to do this is to create a code for each piece or ad placement. Assign a simple set of letters or numbers to the return address, order form, or ad. Another option is to create a special department number keyed to each offer. If customers reply by mail, you can determine their source from the address they used, or you can interpret the code on their order forms. If they call, you can ask them for the department or code number.

Charting the Dollars

When you've collected the responses from a direct mail campaign, chart the income obtained in relation to the key codes. Some mailings may generate larger orders than others. Analyze the response not only in terms of quantity of replies but also in dollars generated per piece mailed. A specific mailing may bring you fewer replies but larger profits. Focus on quality (and net income), not quantity.

Offer a Carrot...for a While

Use an expiration date to give your customers an incentive to buy. This may be a particular date, or a limited time period (such as the next 30 days). Be specific in stating when the offer expires, and mention it at least twice in your pitch. You want your customers to say yes to you today, not to the competition tomorrow.

Thanks to Markus Allen

Stuff It

Don't overlook any opportunity to contact your customers when you send something by mail. Maximize your postage by including brochures, sales flyers, or other announcements when you send out invoices or products.

Dual Impact

Form alliances with companies that are targeting similar customers but are not direct competitors to you. Consider doing joint direct mail campaigns by combining your mailing lists to reach a wider audience.

Double Your List

The easiest way to increase your mailing list is to do a swap with a company trying to reach a market similar to the one you're after. Most exchanges work on a name-for-name basis. Database software eliminates almost all typing, and you can easily merge the new contacts into your main list if you want.

Invite the Reader In

Take time to carefully craft the message on the envelope of your direct mail piece. It can be the deciding factor in whether your message ever reaches the intended recipient's eyes! Since you'll probably have to print a return address on the envelope anyway, think about other messages you'd like to include.

The Power of Color

It may be worth the few extra pennies to send your mailings in brightly colored envelopes. They'll be a visual treat in the pile of incoming mail and can leave a more memorable impact. Some entrepreneurs create laser-printed labels in hot pink, chartreuse, or day-glo yellow to enliven a basic white envelope.

Avoid the Flood

If possible, don't mail from the day after Thanksgiving until the day after Christmas. Avoid letting your marketing message get lost in the sea of holiday catalogs, cards, and other packages.

Thanks to Markus Allen

Resource: *Mail Advertising Hotline (weekly updates), (601) 325-7899*

Chapter 6

Postage & Shipping

Whether it's to deliver products to customers or to reach prospects with a marketing message, businesses rely on postal and shipping services on a daily basis. Frugal entrepreneurs know how to save time and money without cutting back on service. In this chapter, you'll learn how, too.

Stamps or Meter?

The debate is ongoing: is it better to buy stamps or use a postage meter? One side points out that stamps give a more personalized feel to your mail, restating in a subtle way that you value the relationship with the recipient.

Others say that's hogwash. They argue that the contents of the mail are more important than the stamps on it, and the time you save using a postage meter can be spent serving your customers better.

Whichever option you choose, make it work for you. Save time by purchasing quantities of stamps or planning in advance when to fill your postage meter. Invest in a small postal scale and avoid the lines at the post office.

Rolls vs. Sheets

Debate, Part Two: If you choose to use stamps, should you buy them in rolls or in sheets? Buying stamps in rolls saves time, particularly if you use an applicator that can moisten and adhere the stamps easily. On the other hand, stamps in sheets—especially brightly colored or distinctive commemoratives—capture attention and leave a lasting impression.

Meter Specials

If you're thinking about investing in a postage meter, check out the introductory specials that companies sponsor. Many firms offer a 90-day free trial to test the equipment. With proper planning, this could conveniently coincide with a big mailing or PR campaign from your company. You'd enjoy the savings of time and money, and also have the chance to test the equipment's ability to handle a big job.

Two-Bit Handler

If you use stamps in rolls, one of the best bargains in office supplies can be found at your local post office. The U.S. Postal Service (USPS) sells a white plastic stamp dispenser for only a quarter (of course, not too long ago it was a nickel!). The handy unit holds an entire roll of 100 stamps, and keeps them from unraveling and spewing all over your desk. When not in use, it tucks away in a corner of a desk drawer. Ask for one the next time you're at the post office.

Postage Miles

The Postal Service now accepts credit card payment for postage at many post office locations around the country. If postage is one of your company's big expenses, consider charging it to a credit card that gives airline miles. All those stamps and meter fill-ups can add up to a free flight.

Barcoded Savings

Whenever possible, use ZIP+4 coding on your mail, and generate barcodes for your envelopes and mailing labels. (Many new software programs can create the barcodes automatically.) Barcoded mail is processed up to 70 times faster than by hand, and the post office offers quantity discounts for barcoded mail.

Thanks to Markus Allen

Resource: *Mail Advertising Hotline (weekly updates), (601) 325-7899*

Scanner Kindness

Use light-colored envelopes whenever possible. Darker colors reduce the contrast needed for post office computer scanners to operate efficiently—which means your mail could be delayed or lost in processing.

Thanks to Markus Allen

Flat-Rate Savings

Priority Mail from the post office can be a great deal, particularly if you're sending materials that will fit in the standard 2-pound priority letter envelope. The post office uses a flat-rate fee for the envelope, and whatever you can stuff in it will go for the 2-pound charge. For small, heavy items such as books, you can save money over other shipping options.

Thanks to Dan Poynter

Keep Tabs on the Meter

If you're on an automatic renewal agreement with your postage meter service supplier, be sure to analyze the meter's costs to your business at least once a year before your renewal date. With increased usage of faxes and e-mail, it may no longer be worth the investment to you.

Synchronized Scales

From time to time, check your office postal scales with the ones at the post office to make sure yours are still in calibration. Even a small variance can result in wasted postage or returned mail. Select a few common items and mark the exact weight on the outside of each one. Then see if the post office measurements coincide with your own.

Free Envelopes and Cartons

If you buy prestamped envelopes at the post office, you pay only for the postage and the envelope is free. The envelopes are available in a variety of sizes.

If you send something via USPS Priority Mail, they'll provide you with a carton for your package. If you decide to send it by another method (for example, by Parcel Post, which is sometimes cheaper), you can still use the carton. Just gently pull the seam apart, turn the box inside out, and tape it shut. Now you'll have a basic, unmarked cardboard box to use.

Plain Brown Insurance

Using an inside-out carton also is a good way to protect valuables such as computers or electronics you may be shipping back to a manufacturer. The plain brown box is less inviting to thieves than a shiny package touting its contents and value. All the molded Styrofoam packing materials will still fit perfectly, protecting your equipment in transit.

This approach doesn't replace insuring your item, but it can increase the chances of your package arriving at its final destination. It also saves the time of packing the item in another box, or constructing another shipping container.

Labels on Forms

Tired of spending all that time filling out forms for certified or insured mail at the post office? Eliminate the bother by carrying preprinted address labels with you. One lick and you're done!

Thanks to Jon Frost

Peel and Stick

Check out the new self-adhesive stamps available at the post office. They're cleaner, neater, and faster to apply—and few of us miss the gummy aftertaste of the old variety. The no-lick stamps are booming in popularity, and more styles and denominations are being offered all the time.

Fax or Mail?

If you're sending a document that's 5 pages or less, it's probably cheaper to send it by fax, if possible. With telephone rates dropping, faxing is a very cost-effective option, particularly when you tally up the costs of the stamp, the envelope, and the time involved to get it addressed and in the mail. You'll also be delivering the information to your customer in two minutes instead of two to five days.

Drop-Off Savings

Dropping off overnight letters and packages at authorized shipping sites can save you several dollars off the standard rates for pickup service. Make the trip toward the end of the day, in conjunction with other errands, to make the most efficient use of your time.

Let Them Ship It

If you don't ship packages often and haven't established an account with United Parcel Service (UPS), check out your local mailing service center. Many will ship packages for a few dollars over the cost of the shipping fees. This can be an economical solution, since the service center's extra charge is often less than a one-time UPS pickup fee, or the cost of gas and your time to deliver the package to the local UPS office. Another frugal option is to work out a cooperative arrangement with a nearby business that ships on a regular basis.

Dumpster Diving

Frugal entrepreneurs try to avoid buying shipping cartons and packing materials whenever possible. Check out the dumpsters or back lots of local businesses near you that receive packages on a regular basis. You'll be surprised at the amount of material headed for the trash!

Better yet, talk to the store managers and see if you can get the materials before they hit the scuzzy dumpsters. Chances are good that they'll be happy to have you take the materials off their hands and save them the trouble of flattening the cartons.

Peanuts, In and Out

When you get packages filled with Styrofoam packing peanuts, resist the urge to send them off to the landfill. Instead, pour them into a plastic garbage bag and send them back out with your next shipment. The recycling will be gentle on the earth as well as your budget. Even though they're bulky, the peanuts are lightweight and can be stored suspended from a ceiling or in another unused location.

Graded Cartons

When shipping cartons arrive at your business, consider how they might be reused. Once empty, give them a letter or number grade as to their value, and scribble it on a corner. Boxes that are still strong and in good condition receive a high grade, since they will withstand handling and could transport fragile equipment. Containers in poor shape get a low grade and end up being flattened and taken to the recycling center. As boxes accumulate, the grading allows you to determine easily which ones to keep or toss.

Cheaper Than Bubble Wrap

Try using balled-up plastic bags instead of the more expensive bubble wrap to protect fragile items when shipping. The bags come in all shapes and sizes these days—from the dry cleaners, grocery stores, drugstores, or department stores. When balled up, the bags trap enough air to be a good substitute for bubble wrap or packing peanuts.

Thanks to Kevin Donnalley

Tasty Protection

In a pinch about what to use as an inexpensive, light packing material? Try popcorn—the real kind. It's cheap, lightweight, and easy to make as much as you need. The recipient can scatter it on the lawn and treat the local birds.

Online Shipping Info

Detailed shipping information is only a few key strokes away via the Internet. Using your personal computer, you can find correct address information (including ZIP+4 coding), domestic and foreign postal rates, and guidelines on designing business mail.

Once your package is en route, you can track it to see when delivery is anticipated, or if it has already taken place. It's like peering through the digital keyhole to watch the systems that transport millions of packages around the world each day.

Resources: *FedEx, on the Internet at http://www.fedex.com*

United Parcel Service, on the Internet at http://www.ups.com

United States Postal Service, on the Internet at http://www.usps.gov

Chapter 7

Time Management

Of all the resources available to entrepreneurs, none is more valuable than time. Unlike other commodities, this is one that can't be made, bought, bartered, or stolen. It can, however, be used efficiently and wisely— which is what the tips in this chapter are all about.

Activity vs. Achievement

Effective time management begins with an awareness of how you spend your days. Do you squander them on the busyness of business? Are you focusing on activity instead of achievement?

Successful entrepreneurs guard their time like hawks, and devote their energies to specific short- and long-term goals. When deciding how to spend your time, choose with *intent*. Focus on actions that will advance your goals, not merely fill up your days.

List of Seven

To get the most out of each day, create an agenda the night before. At the close of each day, jot down a list of the top seven things you'd like to accomplish the next day. When you come into the office the next morning, you'll be focused and ready to go, instead of wasting the first hour struggling to ramp up and begin.

Creating a list of seven is also a great way to bring closure to a day. The moments you spend reviewing and planning bring perspective, and keep you on target toward your goals.

Why seven? It seems to be the maximum number of things we humans can keep straight in our head. Any more, we become overwhelmed. Any less, we aren't productive enough.

Overlapping Plans

Use overlapping daily, weekly, monthly, and yearly plans for your business. This approach gives you a micro and macro perspective. Set aside time each week to review your master plan for changes, and to see if you've overestimated or underestimated the time needed to reach your objectives.

Thanks to Chuck Galey

Ease into Your Day

Get to work 15 minutes early, and use the time to relax. Running in the door and "jumping into the fire" sets the wrong tone for the day. You'll be more effective if you launch your day with a sense of ease and control.

Thanks to Robert Wagner

Measure Twice, Cut Once

Taking the time to plan and do things right is always cheaper and quicker than doing things in a hurry now to buy some time in order to do things right later. Remember the carpenter's maxim: measure twice, cut once.

Thanks to Evan C. Williams

End-of-Day Closure

In addition to planning your next day's work, take 10–15 minutes at the end of each day to tidy your desk and do some filing. It brings a sense of closure to your day and allows you to return to a neat, inviting work area. Plus, filing in small doses is a lot more palatable than facing an hour's worth once it has piled up.

Know Your Bio-clock

Use your time most effectively by tuning in to your internal biological clock. Be aware of what activities work better for you at different times of the day. Are you someone who springs out of bed each morning, singing? If so, schedule your most demanding tasks for early morning hours.

In contrast, if you struggle through the first hours of the day and really start rolling in midafternoon, tackle activities in the morning that are important but don't require maximum energy or clear thinking. Whatever your personal bio-clock dictates, try to match important tasks to periods when you're most alert.

Play to Your Strengths

Use your time and energy wisely by choosing projects that are a good match for your talents, abilities, and goals. Just because you *can* do something doesn't mean you *need* to do it.

Only Value Need Apply

How much of your day is spent on activities that don't appear to add value? Wage war on those things. Ask yourself, "What percent of my time is spent doing things that no one would miss if I stopped?" Stop doing them! You'll be surprised how much time you can free up.

Thanks to Robert Wagner

Outsource

In the beginning stages, business owners often do every single task themselves. This is a worthwhile approach, because it teaches you every aspect of running a successful company. Once a business is going, however, it is wiser to outsource tasks that take up time and divert energy from the company's main goals.

The rule of thumb: If you can find someone to do tasks for a rate that is less than you can generate for work you do best, hire them. Delegating may be painful at first, but it is often the most economically wise decision in the long run.

Thanks to Lisa Fisher

Be a "Teflon" Delegator

O nce you've hired individuals to do outsourced tasks, resist their tendencies to put some of the work back on you. This often happens by them asking you time-consuming questions or suckering you into doing some related tasks. Successful entrepreneurs develop a "Teflon" delegation style, which deflects all work back to the individuals hired to do it. Be prepared to answer their questions in a concise manner, but avoid taking on their responsibilities.

Magazine Management

A re you overwhelmed by the growing stack of unread magazines in your office? When they arrive, skim the table of contents and rip out articles that interest you. Keep them in a folder to carry in your briefcase to read while commuting or waiting in a restaurant. If you cringe at the thought of destroying the issues, photocopy the contents and mark articles you'd like copied. Remember: Partially read is better than not read at all.

Resource Routing

C reate a file routing slip organized to match your resource file drawers. Keep batches of these slips in all your favorite reading places. Then, when you want to save an article of interest, cut it out and attach a filing slip to it with the correct file folder name checked off. It simplifies the filing, and is a great way to easily see what's in your resource drawer.

Thanks to Lillian Rojas

Stuffing on Hold

If you're doing a large mailing, keep a few envelopes near the telephone and stuff them while you're waiting on hold. Another option is to set up your telephone with a long handset cord or additional extension so you can reach the mailing materials or shipping station. The waiting moments can be more productive, and you won't have to devote specific time to doing mailings.

Thanks to Alison Swerdloff

Plan Your Errand Rounds

Save time, energy, and gasoline by planning a daily circuit of errands to places such as the post office, bank, office-supply store, or copy shop. Visit each in geographic order, with a list in hand, if necessary. By eliminating the backtracking on your route, you'll be finished in half the time.

Line Sleuthing

Being first in a nonexistent line beats being tenth in a long one. Make necessary trips to the bank and post office early in the day, or scope out slack periods. Ask the employees when the slow times are, and plan your visits accordingly. Also, always keep a trade magazine in your car for those unavoidable moments when you're stuck in line, such as at the drive-through window at the bank.

Thanks to Constance Hallinan Lagan

Sign It by Stamp

If you regularly sign a large number of letters, consider getting a rubber stamp of your signature. It's friendlier than a printed signature, and the current models might surprise you with their authenticity. A signature stamp is a reasonable blend of a personalized look and a time-saving approach.

Thanks to Jon Frost

Small Is Beautiful

When tackling a task, always work in measurable, non-overwhelming units for greatest success. Everything we do is actually in units of one—one page at a time, one pile at a time. Small, incremental progress is more efficient than being stymied by lists of large projects on To-Do lists.

Thanks to Paulette Ensign

Master To-Do List

Keep all your tasks on a single master To-Do list. While it may end up being a couple of pages long, a list kept in this manner relieves the stress of worrying if you've forgotten anything important. It also eliminates the possibility of losing small slips of paper containing important tasks.

Rolodex Purge

Purge your Rolodex while on hold on the phone, leaving a paper clip in the last card you reviewed. This accomplishes several things at one time: it cleans your Rolodex, which never reaches a high enough priority to make time to do; minimizes the stress of waiting; and utilizes time appropriately.

Resource: *110 Ideas for Organizing Your Business Life by Paulette Ensign, $6.00, from Organizing Solutions, Inc., (914) 666-6414*

Plan It!

A planned telephone call can take about 7 minutes. An unplanned call will take at least 12 minutes.

Thanks to Paulette Ensign

Slipping By Unnoticed

The biggest culprit in wasted telephone time is being unaware of how long you've been talking. When the day comes to invest in a new telephone, purchase one with a built-in timer readout. At first you'll be shocked at how many minutes are eaten up in making simple calls, or being placed on hold. The timer can be a great tool to help you monitor your phone use and maximize your efficiency.

A more low-tech way to keep calls short is to have an old-fashioned egg timer next to your phone. When a casual conversation begins, invert the hourglass. At the end of three minutes, you can wrap up the call and get back to business.

Important vs. Urgent

When facing a list of tasks, take a moment to decide if each is "important" or "urgent." It is a subtle and revealing distinction.

Important tasks generally have long-term payoff, while urgent tasks may or may not have this value. Many urgent tasks are emergency responses to situations that eat up valuable time with no long-term benefit.

Take a few moments before you embark on a task to determine how much attention and time you should devote to it.

Bank Your Time

You can be significantly more productive if you group similar activities into time segments. For example, avoid telephone interruptions by having a machine, voice mail, or answering service pick up your calls during certain hours. Or "bank" return phone calls for a specific time of the day, and make them during that period.

You can also reduce the frustration of time-wasting telephone tag by leaving a message on your voice mail that states the time period you will be returning calls.

To Meet or Not to Meet?

Before you devote part of your valuable day to a meeting, consider the alternatives. First, ask yourself if your attendance is really necessary. Often a well-planned phone call can accomplish the same end. Phone meetings can be one-on-one or with a group, through the use of a speakerphone.

Instead of sharing lunch, share a phone call. With no travel time, it's much more convenient—and also less fattening!

Agendas Steer the Course

Never walk into a meeting without a clear agenda and goal as to what you want to achieve. Prepare a list of action items you want to accomplish as a result of the meeting, and circulate it to participants, if appropriate. Even if someone else is setting the agenda, prepare your own private list of criteria that will make the meeting successful.

The Caffeine Helps, Too

Breakfast meetings can be very productive. The time is generally "stolen" from sleep hours instead of valuable work hours. A sunup session gets you back to your office early in the day, and the meeting generally doesn't ramble past that last cup of coffee. Plus, breakfast at the best restaurant in town is much less expensive than lunch or dinner.

Thanks to Barbara Sacker

Meeting Over the Wires

An online meeting can often be a great alternative to meeting in person. The bonus? You save travel time, and the meeting may be shorter and more focused. You'll also be able to include participants from around the country—or the world!

Online computer systems enable meetings to be held in "chat" mode in private conference rooms, with individuals typing in their comments so that only invited participants can see. (It also means you'll have a written transcript of the meeting, which can be a handy reference later.)

Videoconferencing facilities are also becoming a more popular rental service in public venues such as photocopy centers. All these options maximize your flexibility and increase your ways to save time.

Chapter 8

Research

In this era of information overload, savvy entrepreneurs understand that the real challenge in doing research is to focus on quality, not quantity. The goal is to find the information you need without getting bogged down in a sea of data, wasting precious time or dollars. This chapter shows how to track down valuable business information while avoiding a costly research budget.

Start General, Not Specific

When asking research professionals for assistance, don't begin with a predetermined notion of the exact end results. It's better to have an idea of the *goal* you have in mind. Let the researchers worry about how to achieve it. If you're too specific with your initial request, you may short-circuit some valuable information they could uncover. Focus on the *what*; allow them to work on the *how*.

Bonus Books

Take advantage of the book clubs that many book stores have set up for regular buyers. If you consolidate your purchases of business books at the same store, you'll see those points add up fast. Use your bonus certificate to get a favorite entrepreneurial book for free.

Thanks to Mary Beth Gehl

Corporate Savings

If your business is incorporated—even as a solo entity—don't overlook the bookstore discounts that may be available to you. Many of the national chains offer an additional 10% off the price of books, audiotapes, or magazines. It's worth asking about at your favorite bookseller, particularly if you're an avid book buyer. Over the course of a year, the savings could make a big difference in your research budget.

Thanks to Carol Vincie

Directories on the Cheap

If the information in the expensive directories you need doesn't change often, try to track down used copies from public or corporate libraries. Many libraries are on an automatic renewal policy to buy the new edition, and older copies often get sold or given away. Ask!

Recycled Media Directories

Marketing and public relations companies often subscribe to expensive annual media directories, since the listings of newspapers, magazines, radio and TV stations, and other media contacts form a core reference tool for their business. Many of the larger firms will discard or recycle older editions.

Make connections with PR professionals and see if you can intercept these valuable guides before they hit the dumpster. Not all of the information will be 100% accurate, but most is still valuable—and the price is right!

Thanks to Greg Godek

Research Buddies

One of the easiest ways to extend your researching abilities is to find one or two other information hounds and agree to be on the lookout for interesting data for each other. It's not that much more difficult to stay aware of one or two other topics, and by tracking, clipping, and e-mailing information for each other, everyone has effectively doubled or tripled their reach.

Avoid Expensive Detours on the Info Highway

The Internet has opened up access to countless databases and other valuable information for entrepreneurs. It's easy to waste a lot of time and money, however, if you aren't familiar with the territory or don't know how to search.

This is particularly true with commercial databases that can charge up to $300/hour. A casual online meander in this high-rent digital neighborhood can do big damage to your budget! Instead, clearly define the parameters of your search, and turn to an experienced online researcher—sometimes as close as your local library. A professional can often complete the task in mere minutes, and save you money.

Searching with Sampler Hours

Many online services (at all price ranges) will often attract new subscribers with several free hours of connect time to explore the service offerings. If you're tackling a research project, consider using these sampler hours to conduct your research—essentially for free. With focus, you can glean a lot of information in a short period of time. You'll also be able to make a wiser decision if the service is worth subscribing to on a regular basis.

Digital Queries

One of the most enjoyable ways to conduct research online is to ask other entrepreneurs for help. Many commercial online services have small business forums with electronic bulletin boards that allow two-way postings. Your questions or requests for information can generate responses from fellow business owners around the world!

Because you are not in a directly competitive geographic area, many subscribers may be willing to share detailed information that they'd be hesitant to openly divulge otherwise, such as pricing or marketing strategies. It's also a great way to find new sources for services and supplies.

Say Yahoo!

The quantity of entrepreneurial information on the Internet is booming. Finding *quality* resources, however, can be challenging. Fortunately, there are several powerful Internet search engines to help you track down information that can be of real value to your business. As you begin your search, choose keywords that define your intended result as clearly as possible. Then add bookmarks of valuable sites to your web browser to guide you on subsequent visits.

Resources: *Yahoo!, on the Internet at http://www.yahoo.com*

InfoSeek, on the Internet at http://www.infoseek.com

Alta Vista, on the Internet at http://www.altavista.digital.com

Online Card Catalog

A growing number of public and university libraries have placed their entire card catalogs online, making them accessible by modem. Call your local library and see if this option is available to you. If so, you can search their complete holdings from your office computer with a local phone call, saving the time and energy of making an in-person visit to see if they have the resources you want.

Thanks to Rebecca Morgan

University Resources

D on't underestimate the wealth of information and assistance available to you from your local college or university. In addition to the library and online services these institutions maintain, area professors may be conducting research on topics that may directly relate to your business. Or they may be willing to undertake research into areas of mutual interest. Entrepreneurial studies is a booming field at many universities these days, and schools are frequently looking to partner with local businesses.

To begin, contact the office of the department you're interested in and introduce yourself. Ask if there are any research studies currently under way in your interest area, or if any professors have a special interest in the topic. Don't be discouraged if you don't link up right away. It may take a while to establish the relationship, but the connection can be very valuable to your business.

Tape It

There are numerous television news digest shows that capsulize important business and financial information. Unfortunately, many of them air during workdays or at other inconvenient or distracting times. If you find these programs to be worthwhile, set your VCR to tape them on a weekly schedule. Set aside time to review the tapes, fast-forwarding during the parts of lesser interest and value.

Join a Control Group

Many trade magazines and newspapers that cater to specific audiences establish a controlled circulation list in addition to paid subscribers. This approach often allows the publication to charge higher ad rates, since a target audience of readers is guaranteed. If you match the demographics of the audience the periodical wants to reach, they may add you to their subscription list for free.

A quick call can determine if it is a controlled circulation publication. If it is, ask how you can be added to the list. Often it's as simple as filling out a form or sending a request on your letterhead.

Teach It and Reap

If you've thought about giving back to your community by teaching a continuing education class, here's even more incentive. If you are a student or educator, you can enjoy great savings on magazine subscriptions. Prices are guaranteed to be the lowest around, and you can get a refund on undelivered issues if you're ever dissatisfied. Hundreds of consumer and business publications are available, including the *Wall Street Journal* and *USA Today* newspapers.

Resources: *American Educational Services, (800) 551-1560*

University Subscription Service, (800) 876-1213

Office in a Briefcase

Mobile entrepreneurs often set up temporary research offices at their local library. The ambiance is quiet and there's no rent to worry about. A briefcase holds stamps, staples, paper, envelopes, and other essentials. A laptop computer and portable printer make the office complete.

Thanks to Steven Tavares

Chapter 9

Professional Advisors & Associations

An entrepreneur's level of success often is tied directly to his or her ability to make connections with others. There are many ways to build a powerful professional network, and the tips in this chapter show you how.

Your Personal Board of Directors

No matter what size your company is, put together a board of advisors. This may comprise fee-based professionals who offer business services such as accounting or legal counsel. Or it may consist of a group of colleagues who share insights as a peer-to-peer relationship.

Many individuals will gladly share their advice on a limited basis in exchange for the personal satisfaction of feeling they played a part in your business success. First you must ask for their participation—and then not abuse their generosity. Express your appreciation and reward them in some personal way.

A personal board of directors can become a powerful extended cheerleading squad for your company. They can steer you clear of business pitfalls, and give you valuable insights from their cumulative experience.

Advisors Worldwide

When you're putting together a team of business advisors, expand your thinking to global proportions. Remember, professionals no longer need to live nearby in order to serve you. Today's technologies of phone, fax, and online systems collapse distance and allow individuals to connect from around the world. This means you can select the very best professionals for your business. Base your choice on the strongest advisors who can serve your business, not on the limitations of where they're located.

Their Advice, Your Nickel

Many professionals are willing to answer quick questions and give free advice on their specialties on a limited basis. The trick is not to abuse this generosity. Do your homework and be prepared to discuss specific questions, not broad issues. Also understand that if the advice becomes very detailed, the professional may suggest that the matter be handled better under a consulting arrangement between the two of you.

When it comes time to ask for advice, make sure you pay for the call. It's not only polite, but it generates good will—and the colleague will be more willing to extend the courtesy in the future.

Thanks Year 'Round

When the holiday season arrives, it's nice to acknowledge the advisors and associates who have helped your business during the year. Keep in mind that business gifts are a deductible expense, up to $25 per recipient. With this price ceiling in mind, many entrepreneurs send gift subscriptions to favorite or unusual magazines. When the issue arrives each month, it says "thanks" from you all over again and reminds the person how much he or she is appreciated.

The Power of Association(s)

One of the best ways to learn more about an industry is to check out the professional associations that serve the field. Think your specialty might be too obscure? Think again! There are nearly 100,000 associations in the United States, devoted to interests ranging from accounting to zoology.

These organizations can provide a wealth of information and contacts for entrepreneurs. Most groups hold an annual meeting and produce regular publications such as a newsletter and an annual directory of members.

The best resource for locating an association in your field of interest is the *Encyclopedia of Associations*. This comprehensive directory lists hundreds of thousands of associations, and gives details on contact information and programs. Nearly every library in the country has one on their reference shelf.

Small Print Says a Lot

When you collect business cards of individuals prominent in a field you're interested in, pay attention to the small type on their business cards. Many times the cards will feature a logo or name of a professional association an individual is affiliated with. It's a great way to discover the key associations in a field, or new organizations you've not previously heard of.

Half-Year for Half Price

Many professional associations structure their annual dues so that all memberships expire at the same time each year. As a result, many groups offer prorated memberships if you join halfway through the year. Before signing up, be sure to ask if an association's dues are based on a calendar year or a rotating annual basis.

By timing your first year's membership properly, you could save some money and still reap the full rewards of the association's services. It will also give you the opportunity to try out an organization before making a larger commitment of time and money.

Thanks to Lucy Mundo

Directory Deadlines

One of the most popular benefits of belonging to an association is participating in an annual membership directory. The listing brings you visibility among other members as well as professionals in the field. When inquiring about an association, be sure to check when their directory goes to press. It may prompt you to send in your membership dues a few months early, and you'll get full value for your investment.

Power in Numbers

Many associations with substantial membership rosters use their power to bargain on members' behalf to get discounts and group rates on a wide variety of services. These might include competitive rates on health and business insurance, discounts on car rentals and office supplies, or free subscriptions to business publications. Sometimes it makes sense to join an association that offers a good service, even if the organization may be unrelated to your field. Your savings can more than cover the membership dues.

Have an Agenda

Before attending a professional conference or annual meeting, prepare a list (either mentally or on paper) of the top three to five items you'd like to accomplish. For example, on the trip to the event, take time to review the conference itinerary and decide if there is a particular individual with whom you want to connect, certain information you want to learn, or a product from a specific company you want to investigate.

In the quiet of a plane, train, or bus, you'll be able to create a clearer focus of your personal and professional goals for the event—before being distracted by registration details, settling into the hotel, or catching up with colleagues you haven't seen in a while. With an agenda in hand, you'll get more value out of every conference.

Schedule Breathing Room

When attending a conference or convention, allow some unplanned time in your schedule. Experienced entrepreneurs understand that some of the most valuable connections can happen in the hallways or hotel lobby, in those in-between moments during a conference or meeting. If you leave some time open for the unexpected, you'll be able to take advantage of opportunities when they arise.

Time to Debrief

Upon returning from a conference, it's natural to jump right back into the fray of daily office operations and push the meeting handouts and other content into some bottom file drawer or office shelf. But studies show that if you don't use new information within 72 hours after learning it, chances are you won't use it at all.

If possible, schedule part of the first day back in the office to assimilate what you've learned and to put into practice a few key ideas. It's a great time to sort out business cards and create a follow-up plan for maximizing new contacts. A few hours spent wisely often can bring all of your conference efforts to fruition, and increase the chances that your investment of time and money will pay off.

Capture "Keepers"

When attending a conference with inspiring programs and speakers, it's tempting to take pages and pages of notes. Unfortunately, these notes often end up stashed in some soon-forgotten notebook, never to be referred to again. A better approach is to focus on capturing "keepers"—those few ideas that strike you as most important and that can make a difference in your business.

Limit your page to the things you actually plan on doing something about, and write only enough to remind you of the focus. After the conference, put your keeper pages in a notebook near your computer. Review them when you are on hold, or use a Post-It note with your top three keepers on it as a reminder on your daily calendar.

Your keeper system will soon have much greater impact than pages and piles of notes. Remember, it's not how many good ideas you learn. It's how well you use the ones that count!

Thanks to Terry Paulson, author of They Shoot Managers, Don't They? *(Ten Speed Press, (800) 841-2665)*

Create an Action List

Another important list to create at a conference is a one-page action list of tasks to follow-up on once you're back in your office. For instance, this may include reminders to send materials to new contacts, or details on a new product or service to check out. Keeping these items on a separate sheet or card makes the list easy to refer to, and sets it apart from the other pages of your conference notes. Back in your office, it becomes a handy To-Do list of promises to keep.

Name Badge on the Right

Experienced conference attendees know that there's only one place to wear your name badge: high on your right lapel area. Placement here makes networking much easier, since most individuals extend their right hand to introduce themselves or say hello. As you're shaking hands, you can clearly see the person's name, smile, and make eye contact in one graceful motion. Once you're aware of this, you'll wish everyone wore their name badge on their right side.

Power Partners

Introducing a close colleague to a new contact can be a positive and powerful experience for everyone involved. You get a chance to "brag" about your friend in ways that he or she would never be brash enough to do. The comments also carry much more credibility, since they come from you and not the person being introduced.

When making the introduction, show enthusiasm in your voice. Mention not only the individual's accomplishments but also something that reveals his or her personality.

Your actions not only will give a boost to your power partner, they also will reflect favorably on your own standing as someone who knows fascinating and influential people. It's a win/win situation that can have a lasting impact on everyone involved.

Resources: How to Work a Room *and* The Secrets of Savvy Networking *by Susan RoAne (Warner Books, (212) 522-6982)*

Variety Is the Spice

When attending an event, it's tempting to socialize with colleagues you know. By making a point to vary your luncheon companions and the individuals you chat with during breaks, you'll expand your personal and professional network.

Indirect Introductions

It's a situation we've all been in: You've been engaged in conversation with someone for at least five minutes, and you can't remember their name. Suddenly a spouse or colleague walks up to join the conversation. You panic, wondering what to do.

Here's one solution, although it takes a savvy partner to pick up on the situation and make it work smoothly. Turn to the name-unknown person, smile, and prepare to introduce the person who's just joined the conversation by saying, "Oh, have you met...." The "joiner" then immediately smiles, sticks out a hand, and says his or her own name to the still-unknown person, completing the introduction. Most often, the unknown person will respond with a smile and a name. Puzzle solved—and you make a mental note to remember the person's name the next time you meet!

Chapter 10

Money Matters

Managing financial matters well is at the heart of being a frugal entrepreneur. Smart business owners understand that saving money is only the first step. This chapter offers specific ideas on how to make your money work as hard for your business as you do.

Budgets Bring Freedom

Many new small business owners try to "wing it" when it comes to budgeting—with disastrous results. In contrast, seasoned entrepreneurs understand that preparing a financial forecast is well worth the effort.

Begin with your best estimates, and err on the conservative side. Over the course of a few months and years, income and expense patterns often emerge, making it easier to budget. Allocating funds to categories such as "unexpected opportunities" or "crisis cushion" will give you the flexibility to respond to unplanned situations yet maintain a stability in your business. You'll save time, energy, and money because you won't be pulled off track from your main business focus.

Per Hour or Project?

When reviewing a project for a potential client, decide in advance if you will be billing by the hour or by the project. Clients with a fuzzy definition of what they want to achieve may make many changes along the way—and if you're billing by the project, your profit may evaporate!

In contrast, clients with a clearly defined project may feel more comfortable with project-based pricing. This approach frees you from the time-consuming chore of tracking details. When adopting either method, be sure there is a clear understanding of what is expected for the agreed-upon price. Work beyond the project definition is then billed as additional hours or as a subsequent project.

Thanks to Ann Cook

An Easy Paper Trail

One of the best ways to simplify your bookkeeping is to leave a paper trail of your income and expenses. Try to pay by check or credit card as often as you can, and keep personal and business funds separate. Using this approach, your bank account statements and credit card bills will provide you with an easy way to track your finances with minimal bookkeeping. Some credit cards even provide year-end summaries of expenses by categories.

Slippery Dollars

Set a goal where your money *has* to go. Otherwise, it just goes!

Thanks to Ann Cook

The Early Bird Gets...

If your cash flow allows, take advantage of the early-payment or prepayment discounts your suppliers may offer you. With interest rates at meager levels and many banks not offering interest at all on business checking accounts, the savings of 2–5% on your bill may be a wise financial move.

The Bill Collectors Don't Care

Paying bills can be painful enough. Why spend money on envelopes? Save any envelope—in good condition—that you can get your hands on. You can use it later for paying bills that don't come with their own return envelope. Just attach a label over the old mailing address, and make sure no bar codes or other information that may confuse the post office show through.

Thanks to Chuck Galey

Choosing a "Business" Credit Card

You don't need to spend extra money to get a "corporate" credit card. Just designate one (or more) of the cards you currently have for business use only. (Remember, the IRS frowns on business owners mixing personal and business finances.) When it is used only for business purposes, the credit card's annual fees are tax-deductible as a business-related expense.

Amazing Grace, Frugal Style

Savvy frugal entrepreneurs with several credit cards know the monthly closing dates of each credit card billing period. They also choose cards with a grace period—ones that accrue interest starting at the end of the billing period instead of on the date of purchase. By making charges early in the card's monthly cycle, they get "free" rental of money for several weeks before the bill becomes due.

Thanks to David Tisdale

Shop for Credit Card Interest Rates

Credit card companies vary greatly in the way they calculate interest. Many companies offer enticing initial rates, then increase them dramatically after 6 or 12 months. Entrepreneurs who carry at least a $1,000 balance may opt for a permanent low-interest card tied to the prime rate. Although it has a heftier annual fee (approximately $90), the long-term savings in interest charges may be worth it.

Resources: *Prime for Life Credit Card, Wachovia Bank, (800) 842-3262*

CardTrack, RAM Research Group, (800) 344-7714; monthly guide offering information on hundreds of the best credit card deals; sample issue is $5.00

The Payoff's in the Perks

Credit card companies are becoming very competitive in the value-added perks they're offering to lure new customers. Choose a card not only for its interest rate but also for the extra benefits it can bring. For example, using a "gold" card when you purchase an item with a warranty often adds an additional year of warranty coverage. Many also offer 90 days of theft protection and reimbursement. Others offer cash back on purchases made with their cards. By comparing the alliances a credit card company has made with other firms, you can determine if the expenses of their card's annual fees and interest are a worthwhile trade-off for the benefits it can bring your business.

Thanks to Kim Mosley

Flying on the Ground

One of the most effective ways to rack up frequent flyer miles is to focus on *one* airline as your preferred carrier. Find credit cards, hotels, car rental agencies, restaurants, and other companies that have an arrangement to offer that airline's frequent flyer miles in exchange for using their services. This "double-dipping" and consolidating can help you achieve mileage bonuses and other premiums, and will enable you to accumulate mileage for free tickets faster. Also, when it comes time to buy that expensive piece of office equipment, use a credit card that will give you frequent flyer credits. Particularly with big purchases, the miles can add up fast!

Thanks to Mary Beth Gehl

Move Accounts Receivable to Plastic

To increase pay-up rates on invoices, place a brightly colored sticker at the bottom of the invoice that says: "Just a friendly reminder to let you know that you can transfer your balance to VISA, MasterCard, or American Express." Be sure to include your phone number so customers know where to call.

Resource: The Manager's Intelligence Report, *Ragan Communications,* *(312) 335-0037*

Painless Debt-Busting

Small increases in your payments on credit card debt can have a big impact. On a typical credit card balance of $2,000, adding just $25 a month to the regular payment can save up to $6,000 over the payoff period.

Thanks to Marc Eisenson and Nancy Castleman

Tax Stash

A void the cash crunch that comes at tax time by setting aside a cash reserve for taxes. Putting this money in an interest-bearing account means that it's increasing in value until the IRS deadline date—as well as giving you peace of mind that your tax obligations are covered. A reserve fund also brings stability when your business cycle slows down and cash flow is low. Planning ahead saves money on high interest rates that an emergency loan or credit card advance often carries.

Thanks to Chuck Galey

Bank Shopping

Many entrepreneurs overlook the fact that banks are businesses, too. They have various "products" to sell such as savings and checking accounts, CDs, safe deposit boxes, ATM cards, credit lines, and loans.

Determine what services your small business needs, and prepare a paper grid listing the features, benefits, and pricing of services by area banks. Don't forget to factor in the "chemistry" of friendly and helpful bank personnel. You'll be surprised at the range of costs and savings. It pays to shop around.

Money on Sale

Many banks offer periodic "sales" on credit lines and loans by offering them at reduced interest rates or with no additional set-up fees. Bank managers have discretion to waive fees or to offer lower rates—but you'll only get this special treatment if you ask.

Annual Fee Review

Once a year, take time to review and compare bank fees for services such as monthly maintenance, check writing, ATM withdrawals, or checks returned for insufficient funds. You can often save hundreds of dollars by negotiating lower fees or by changing banks.

Thanks to Constance Hallinan Lagan

Suppliers as Your Banker

It pays to establish a good relationship with your suppliers. Favorable credit terms with key suppliers can translate into big savings for your small business. For example, payments stretched out over several months can do wonders for your cash flow. It also means you won't have to rely on credit lines or loans that would rack up interest charges.

Shop around for suppliers willing to offer fair pricing and flexible payment terms. When you find a good one, treat your relationship like gold—because in many ways it is!

Credit Line vs. Loan

Save yourself some money by establishing a credit line instead of getting a traditional bank loan. A credit line is a "pool" of approved money that sits waiting until you need it.

The bonus: Credit line interest does not start accruing until the funds hit your checking account, and you can access only a portion of your credit line instead of the whole lump sum. This can mean considerable savings in interest charges, and greater flexibility in your financial planning.

Credit Line Transfers

Many banks have established minimum amounts for credit line transfers. If you need only a few hundred dollars and the minimum transfer is $10,000, you'll be accruing expensive interest charges on unnecessary funds.

See if your bank will cut the minimum transfer amount in half, which will reduce your interest fees. Many bank managers have the authority to do this. If not, consider moving the money temporarily over to an interest-bearing account, such as a savings account.

While not the ideal solution—since the credit line interest you'll be paying is generally higher than the savings account interest you'll be earning—it beats having the unused funds costing you any more money than is necessary.

Checks by Mail

Don't waste money by buying expensive checks through your bank. Instead, order them by mail at half the cost! Mail-order check firms offer a wide variety of designs from which to choose, ranging from cute to more sedate business styles. You'll need to send a voided check with the appropriate bank routing numbers for your initial order. Many firms then accept reorders by phone or fax.

Thanks to Constance Hallinan Lagan

Resources: *Checks in the Mail, (800) 733-4443*

Current Business Check Products Division, (800) 667-2439

Designer Checks, (800) 239-9222

The Check Gallery, Inc., (800) 354-3540

Or, No Checks at All

If you find paying bills by check a chore, and dislike the time and expense of writing checks, stuffing envelopes, licking stamps, and making trips to the post office, an electronic check payment service may be a frugal investment for you. These services send payments electronically, transferring funds from your account on the date you specify payments are to be made. Laser-printed checks are mailed to individuals or companies not yet linked to an electronic network.

You can choose the option of paying with your touch-tone telephone or via your personal computer. Both options use security codes to make sure that only you have access to your account. The fees are often less than the cost of stamps, not to mention the time savings.

Resource: *CheckFree Payment Services, (800) 882-5280 or on the Internet at http://www.checkfree.com*

Credit Card Security

Looking for an easy way to keep track of all your credit card numbers in case the cards get stolen? Place all your cards face down on the photocopier glass, and push the button. Bingo! You've just created a master list of all your cards, including expiration dates and the names of the issuing banks.

The next step is to write down the toll-free numbers you'll need to call to report a theft, and to store this sheet in a safe, but accessible, place.

Contribute Early

If you can, contribute to your IRA or other retirement program early in the year. For example, retirement contributions for the 1997 tax year can be made until tax filing day on April 15, 1998. Savvy entrepreneurs, however, make at least part of their contribution in January 1997, gaining almost 16 months of interest. Over time, this strategy can have a significant positive impact on your retirement investment as interest accrues. Check with your financial and tax advisors to see how you can maximize your savings.

The Rule of 72

Want to know how fast your money will grow, after taxes, over any given time frame? Divide the number 72 by the rate of growth or return. The answer indicates how many years it will take for the amount saved to double using that rate of growth. For example, an investment returning 8% doubles in 9 years (72 divided by 8), while one returning 6% takes 12 years to double.

This process can also be used to help you determine what rate of growth you need to double your money over a set time period. For instance, a 10-year investment will have to return 7.2% yearly if you want your money to double in those 10 years, while an investor hoping to double his or her investment in 12 years will require only a 6% return.

The lesson is to invest early and often. Then the power of compounding interest can be put to work.

Thanks to Irv Blackman

Chapter 11

Staff

The individuals involved in a business give it its spark and life. Dedicated workers can help a company soar to great heights, while careless ones can cause it to falter or fail. Whether you hire employees or partner with solo professionals, the tips in this chapter will guide you in managing one of your most valuable business resources.

Interns

If your company is looking for a way to bring on extra help without straining your budget, check with local colleges and universities about the possibility of using interns. Advanced students in business and marketing programs are often looking for work experience, both to expand their knowledge and to establish some credentials on their résumés. Some will work as unpaid staff; others require compensation, but it often can be at a reasonable rate.

Keep in mind that working with an intern is a two-way street. In exchange for their labor, interns deserve an educational experience that is interesting and well rounded. Your role as boss will also include being a teacher, explaining how the intern's activities fit into the overall workings of your business as well as the larger business community.

An internship program can also be a good screening method for prospective employees. Even if the individual does not come on board later as a staff member, he or she can be a valuable resource as an independent contractor for special projects.

Help Wanted

L ooking for the best way to find prospective interns or college-age employees? Volunteer to give a presentation on your company or another related business topic to a business or marketing class at a nearby college or university. It's a great way to "advertise" your business while giving something back to the community. The best students will likely be motivated enough to contact you about work, and you'll be able to select from among them.

Thanks to Betty Hunter

Doing Good with Staff Dollars

W hen faced with a simple, repetitive, light-manufacturing task—such as stuffing products in envelopes or boxes—consider using area training centers for physically or mentally challenged individuals. These programs can deliver quality work, and your business dollars can have the extra impact of helping those in need in your community.

Thanks to Barbara Hemphill

The Fine Art of Delegation

Entrepreneurs have personal comfort levels when it comes to delegation. Many freely turn over major projects to outside help, while others wince at letting even the simplest task out of sight. Delegation is a skill, not an inborn character trait.

The best delegators are those who continually stretch their comfort level by letting go of a little more control. They weigh the risks of a project not getting done exactly as they would do it or not getting done at all. Where's your comfort level?

When to Delegate?

A simple question can clarify any confusion about delegation: Can *anyone else* do this task besides me? If the answer is yes, delegate. Save your time and energy by focusing on activities that *only you* can do. Too often, entrepreneurs believe their hands-on attention is essential. As you continue to ask this question, you'll gain clarity on what your strengths are, and where you can invest your time, energy, and money most effectively.

Hire Wisely

Research shows that more than 50% of new hires will leave before the end of their first year. Taking time to screen potential employees or contractors carefully in the initial stages will be worth it in the long run. Avoid the frustration and expense of always training new staff by choosing well when hiring.

Incentives Instead of Salary

New ventures often cannot afford expensive salaries to hire top-notch employees—yet these staff members can have a profound effect on a company's success. You can frequently hire someone more expensive than you can afford by offering a percentage of the business profits. This increases the compensation value to the employee. It also instills a sense of dedication, since the new hire's salary is directly tied to the company's future.

Thanks to Howard Wolf

Ask the New Kid on the Block

Don't underestimate the value that new employees can bring to your company. Because they are not steeped in the techniques and traditions of your business, newcomers often offer unexpected perspective.

When it comes time to explain a project to a new employee, begin by stating the end goal in mind instead of the detailed method of how *you* would tackle the task. Using this approach, you won't short-circuit any good ideas.

Once this new team member has outlined his or her proposed method, compare notes. You can then create the best technique to achieve the desired end. Valuable insights can come from viewing things with a fresh pair of eyes.

Put It in Writing

Whether you're hiring independent contractors or employees, it pays to have both parties put in writing their understanding and expectations of the position. A simple work contract can spell out responsibilities and establish clear communication. The contract can also be a valuable reference document for performance appraisal.

The Problem, Not the Person

When you need to correct a staff member's mistake, choose your words carefully. Emphasize the error, not the person committing it. Try to use the pronoun "we" instead of "you," and speak about the intended result instead of the failed attempt. This approach will create a smoother dialogue between you, and help the staff member keep an open mind to constructive criticism.

The Shadow

In some situations, an effective way of training a new staff member is to ask them to "shadow" you for two or three days, tagging along on your business appointments and writing down observations and questions. This can provide a good overview of the scope of your business and the positive impact they can have on it. At the end of the few days, spend time debriefing and answering their questions.

Thanks to Terri Kabachnick

Transition Status

O nce an employee has announced his or her intention to leave, "short-timer's syndrome" can set in, resulting in an increased drop in productivity. As an employer, you can maximize these remaining weeks by asking the staff person to create a status report of all unfinished business, listing projects to be completed and the person who will likely take them on. This provides a valuable overview of pending actions, ensuring that momentum is not lost on important projects and that follow-up can proceed smoothly.

An "Inside" Job Description

A nother valuable transition document is a detailed job description of the soon-to-be-departing employee, prepared by the person who knows it best— that employee. This "brain dump" of the person's job can be relatively painless to create, since it is a recap of what the employee knows by heart. It can be a priceless document, however, since it captures the subtle nuances of a job. These details often take months to discover, and can give a significant head start to any new employee.

Ask to have the document prepared on disk. That way, you can review and edit the content to make sure it represents how you feel the new staff member should be trained.

Hiring Your Kids

Hunting for someone to help out with cleaning, filing, mailing, or other chores in your small business? Don't overlook one of the best sources for semiskilled labor around—your children. It is perfectly legal to pay your kids for their efforts and to deduct the costs as a business expense, even if the youngsters are in grade school.

The key is to pay them a fair market wage—that is, no $20/hour work for an eight-year-old sweeping the floor (no matter how precocious he or she may be!). It's also important to keep a log of when they worked and the tasks completed.

The tax advantages can also be significant. If children are under 18, their wages are not subject to Social Security tax. Also, their earned income can equal the standard deduction (nearly $4,000) before their wages become subject to federal income tax. They also may be eligible to open an IRA and boost their tax-free earnings even more. Check with your tax advisor for details.

Chapter 12

Travel

Business owners who spend a lot of time on the road know that travel costs can put a sizable dent in any budget. You want to economize, yet cutting back on things that help your trips be productive can be foolish frugality. This collection of travel tips will help you keep your company going, even while you're out of the office.

Let Your Fingers Leapfrog Lines

When your flight has been canceled, avoid the long lines of frantic people scrambling to get rerouted. Instead, head for the nearest bank of pay phones and call the airline. The agents on the other end of the phone will be accessing the same computer as those behind the counter, and can give you options without your having to contend with the environment of dozens of irate passengers. It's a good reason to keep the toll-free numbers of your regular airlines in a handy spot.

Ship It, Don't Schlep It

If you're traveling with particularly bulky or heavy items, consider having them shipped to your hotel or other destination ahead of time. Often the freight costs are worth the convenience of not having to worry or make on-the-spot arrangements for transport. And it sure beats lugging all that stuff through airports.

Delivered Wheels

Arriving in an unfamiliar city at night and plan to rent a car? Think about having the vehicle delivered to your hotel instead, where it can be waiting for you when you arrive. Many car rental companies can arrange this service. It may be a better choice than trying to navigate unknown streets when you're tired and in a new city.

Silence Is Golden

There's one phrase that's almost guaranteed to save you money when you're making travel plans. When calling around for the best fares on airline tickets, car rentals, hotels, or other services, be sure to begin your conversations by saying, "I'm shopping for... (a plane ticket, rental car, etc.)." This is a way of letting the travel provider understand that price is important to you.

If the travel professional comes back with a price that you feel is too high, pause and ask, "Is that the best there is? I was really hoping to get something a bit lower." Then comes an important step: *stop talking.* Let the request hang in the air, and become the agent's concern. Most likely, the agent will continue the hunt and somehow turn up a fare or rate that's lower than the first one quoted to you.

It's remarkable how many times this approach works. During it all, it's important to keep a professional and cheery demeanor. When you're through, be sure to tell the travel provider how much you appreciate the help.

Thanks to Jim Rhode

Hotel Discounters

Frugal entrepreneurs understand that hotel owners would rather have their rooms filled at night than remain empty. Many rooms can be obtained at discounted rates through companies called consolidators. These firms contract with leading hotels in major cities to buy rooms in large quantities for resale, often at rates lower than the hotel would charge. When shopping for a lower hotel rate, a quick phone call to a consolidator may save you some money.

Resources: *Express Reservations, (800) 356-1123*

Hotel Reservations Network, (800) 964-6835

Quikbook, (800) 789-9887

Room Exchange, (800) 846-7000

The Power of a Sigh

Never underestimate the impact a sigh can bring to your negotiations for lower travel prices. It signals your disappointment that the price isn't any better, and that you expected more. Additional explanations usually aren't needed, and the travel professional on the other end of the phone often will continue looking for a less expensive alternative.

In person, a sigh coupled with a shake of the head can be particularly powerful. Try it the next time you're chasing a bargain.

Music in Your Ears

In case you haven't noticed, the headset jacks on larger planes used for transcontinental flights are identical to those on your personal cassette player. This means you can jack into music or movies wearing your own lightweight headset. Some airlines charge you the movie fee even if you use your own equipment, while others let you enjoy music at no charge. A few travelers pay the movie fee and still use their own earphones, since they prefer them over bulky and uncomfortable airline headsets.

Variety in the Air

If the thought of another airline meal makes you cringe, take the time to investigate the meal options offered by your favorite airline. Nearly two dozen alternatives are available at no additional cost. They range from dietary meals (e.g., low-salt, low-calorie, low-cholesterol, gluten-free, or non-lactose) to choices for religious sects (e.g., Kosher, Hindu, or Muslim). Passengers also can often obtain seafood, fresh fruit, or vegetarian selections.

Airlines report that only about 20% of customers ask for a special meal, even though the request can be made as late as 6 hours before a flight's scheduled departure time (12 hours for Kosher meals).

There's no reason to sit through rubber chicken again! Gain the envious stares of your fellow passengers—pick up the phone and order your special meal the night before you fly. It's free for the asking.

Multiple Airports

If you live in or are flying into a major metropolitan area served by more than a single airport, you often can obtain discounted pricing on travel by comparison shopping. Airlines frequently run promotions or specials for trips to and from selected airports. It pays to ask if there is a cheaper fare into or out of another regional airport serving your needs.

Also, if a fare is less at one airport but you prefer using another, ask the airline if it can match the competitive price. Many times the agents can grant your request—but you have to ask them to do it.

Insider Insights

If you'll be doing business in a city and you'd like to do some pretravel research on the business community climate, restaurants, or other special attractions, there's an easy way to get expert advice. Call the best hotel you know of in the city and ask for the concierge desk. In moments you'll have access to one of the top industry insiders about the best of everything the city has to offer.

Thanks to Lisa Fisher

Personal Miles

When it comes time to cash in your frequent flyer miles, use them strategically. Pick a flight that would be expensive—perhaps because of the distance, a remote destination, or a shortened time frame before you must fly.

Clever entrepreneurs who are tax-savvy try to use frequent flyer miles for personal trips, since they know that business travel is a deductible expense.

Coupon Central

Business owners' mailboxes are filled on a regular basis with discount coupons and other travel incentives designed to lure your travel dollars and build your allegiance. Many of these promotions can be money savers, *if* you can locate the flyers when you need them.

The key is to create a central file in which to store the coupons and other literature. Keep it handy and review it before you're ready to make your next travel plans. Chances are, a saved coupon can be redeemed for either better service (such as an upgrade) or a discount.

Fly-In Meetings

Many airline clubs have meeting rooms at major airports that are available for rent at reasonable hourly rates, even if you're not a club member. With proper scheduling, this can be an efficient way of connecting with clients in a professional environment while on the road.

Maps and More

Founded in 1902, the American Automobile Association (AAA) offers member services such as discounts on lodging and car rentals, travel and reservation assistance, AAA VISA and MasterCard services, maps and tour books, and their famed emergency roadside service, reached from anywhere in the United States at (800) AAA-HELP.

For information on signing up and to access membership services, check the business listings section of your local phone book under AAA. You'll find local numbers in your area for recorded weather reports and road conditions, automated map ordering, even someone to help you with a membership application. Frugal entrepreneurs know that the cost of a single towing charge if your car breaks down on the road could be worth the annual membership fee.

Pre-Trip Checklist

In the rush before leaving on a trip, it's easy to over look an important task or critical item. Experienced travelers know how handy a pre-trip checklist can be. Some create them as a handwritten To-Do list that changes for every trip, while others generate a more structured form on their computer that they update and print out before traveling.

Whichever approach you use, make the list as complete as possible and include even the most obvious tasks and items. Seasoned "road warriors" know that sometimes the simple things left behind can cause the biggest headaches or inconveniences.

Suitcase to Go

If you find yourself traveling on a regular basis, you can save time packing and unpacking by keeping a spare suitcase packed and ready to go. Many veteran travelers invest in an extra set of toiletries, a small hair dryer, and other travel items. These are kept right in the suitcase to save space and packing time.

You can expand this concept to other travel items as well, such as a spare set of undergarments, hosiery, sleepwear, or basic clothing. Choose which approach works for you and you'll eliminate the frantic predeparture realization that your must-have travel item is either depleted, broken, or in the dirty laundry basket.

Check-In Check

When you're checking into a hotel, take a few moments while the bellman is with you to make sure everything in your room works. This includes heating, air conditioning, windows, lighting, TV remote control, radio, alarm clock, and door lock. There's nothing worse than discovering that your bedside light doesn't work just as you're ready to do some late-night reading.

Also check to be sure you have an ample supply of towels and clothes hangers. A few minutes spent as you're checking in can save you an hour of aggravation and waiting later.

In-House Printer

Looking for a way to lighten your load when traveling? Take your laptop, but leave the printer at home. Many of today's better hotels offer business centers, complete with high-speed photocopiers, printers, and secretarial services.

If the hotel's business services are closed for the night, an easy way to get a printout is to hook your laptop up to your in-room telephone line and send your document to the hotel's fax number. Voilà, a hard copy of your important file will be waiting for you at the hotel desk just a few moments later, often at no charge.

Modem Mania

Connecting to online computer services from hotel room phones with your laptop can be notoriously frustrating. The process is routinely filled with numerous attempts, multiple disconnects, and intermittent service. The shock comes when you check out and the hotel charges you for every call. It's not unusual for this to add an additional $10 or more to your bill.

Many hotels will be flexible in their policies and remove these charges if you ask them to do so. The key is to keep a log of how many failed attempts and disconnects occurred. When faced with a list on paper—even a simple scrawled one—the desk staff is much more willing to waive the fees.

Phone Home

If your business takes you on the road frequently, and you need to check in with the office or your home on a regular basis, consider getting a personal toll-free number. Rates have dropped considerably in recent years, and many services have eliminated monthly fees or minimum charges.

Your personal toll-free number can piggyback on any existing line, so there's no additional wiring necessary. The costs are often less than using calling cards, and you'll save time by not having to dial in extensive strings of numbers.

Resource: *Paulin Communications, (800) 324-9449*

Room to Spare

The next time you're facing a bulging suitcase at the end of a trip, remember the humorous truism that dirty clothes always end up requiring more space than clean ones. It's the reason seasoned travelers always tuck a lightweight collapsible nylon suitcase into their original bag before they depart. In addition to being a handy way to save time during homeward-bound packing, the spare bag can be filled with new purchases or bulky items such as sweaters.

Trip Pouch

Remember those zippered pencil pouches in colorful plastic that were so much a part of grade-school years? In adult life, they can take on new meaning and usefulness as trip organizers. Assorted travel papers can be gathered and stored in one place, including tickets, shuttle and limousine schedules, passports, foreign currency, small bills for bellman tips, and other items.

The pouches are also a helpful collection point for all travel-related receipts, making it easy to complete tax records or expense reports. If you choose a clear plastic pouch, you'll be able to see its contents at a glance—but so will others, so take care.

Resources

Frugal entrepreneurs understand that the search for ways to save time, energy, and money never ends. To supplement the resources cited in the main pages of this book, here are some other valuable publications to enhance your frugal mindset.

BOOKS

Beating the System by Larry Roth. Kansas City, Mo.: Living Cheap Press, 1995. $17.95. (816) 523-3161

A treasury of experienced, opinionated, and practical advice about how to save enough money to live without a job.

Choose to Reuse by Nikki and David Goldbeck. Woodstock, N.Y.: Ceres Press, 1995. $15.95. (914) 679-5573

More than 2,000 detailed resources of services, products, programs, and charitable organizations that foster reuse.

Guerrilla Marketing Handbook by Jay Conrad Levinson and Seth Godin. New York: Houghton Mifflin, 1994. $16.95. (800) 225-3362

Hundreds of ideas, contacts, and resources to get maximum marketing from a minimal budget.

How to Drive the Competition Crazy by Guy Kawasaki. New York: Hyperion, 1995. $22.95. (800) 759-0190

Written with a delightfully irreverent David-beats-Goliath approach, this book celebrates the use of clear thinking, shrewdness, guts, and hard work to trounce one's competitors.

How to Keep Your Hard-Earned Money by Henry Aiy'm Fellman. Boulder, Colo.: Solutions Press, Inc., 1996. $17.95. (800) 211-0544

A clear, easy-to-use handbook that presents surefire tax-saving methods for self-employed people in all professions.

Marketing Bootcamp by Arnold Sanow and J. Daniel McComas. Dubuque, Iowa: Kendall/Hunt Publishing, 1994. $29.95. (800) 228-0810

A collection of 85 tools, techniques, and strategies to boost your marketing impact and business profits.

Marketing on a Shoestring by Jeff Davidson. New York: John Wiley & Sons, Inc., 1994. $14.95. (800) CALL-WILEY

Techniques and strategies for low-cost, high-impact marketing for your products or services.

101 Home Office Success Secrets by Lisa Kanarek. Hawthorne, N.J.: Career Press, 1993. $9.95. (800) CAREER-1

A collection of informative, practical solutions to common problems facing individuals who have home offices.

101 Tax Saving Ideas by Randy Gardner and Julie Welch. Kansas City, Mo.: Wealth Builders Press, 1995. $14.95. (800) 410-1829

Comprehensive tax tips on investments, itemized deductions, small business strategies, and retirement planning in easy-to-understand language.

Organizing Options by the San Francisco Bay Area Chapter of the National Association of Professional Organizers. San Francisco: NAPO, 1994. $14.95. (415) 281-5681

A compendium of ideas, insights, and practical tips on home, office, and personal management topics from professional organizers.

Postal Business Companion by the United States Postal Service. Alexandria, Va.: Braddock Communications, 1994. Free.

A handy guide that covers small business postal services, business mail management, proper format for business correspondence, and appendices and glossaries of postal terms and data. Available from your local USPS Business Center (check the blue pages of your telephone directory).

6 Steps to Free Publicity by Marcia Yudkin. New York: Plume/Penguin, 1994. $9.95. (800) 331-4624

A top-notch guide on how to generate powerful publicity for your business, for free.

Small Business, Big Savings by Laura Teller and Warren R. Schatz. New York: HarperCollins Publishers, Inc., 1995. $14.95. (800) 625-7764

A one-stop guide with names, product line descriptions, and contact information of companies that offer significant savings on office supplies, furniture, travel, computers, consulting, marketing, and other business products and services.

The Tightwad Gazette by Amy Dacyczyn. New York: Villard Books/ Random House, Inc., 1993. $9.99. (800) 733-3000

The classic guide with hundreds of tips, tricks, and strategies promoting thrift as a viable alternative lifestyle.

Work Tips by Patricia Katz. Regina, Saskatchewan: The Leader-Post
Carrier Foundation, Inc., 1995. $14.95. (306) 242-0795;
(306) 242-0795 (fax)

Loaded with down-to-earth tips to streamline your work, including
ways to organize your time, ideas, activities, and surroundings.

Your Money or Your Life by Joe Dominguez and Vicki Robin.
New York: Viking/Penguin, 1992. (800) 331-4624

Presents a 9-step program for financial freedom based on a new
way of looking at earning, spending, and saving money.

NEWSLETTERS

Bootstrappin' Entrepreneur, editor/publisher: Kimberly Stanséll. This
publication is billed as "the newsletter for individuals with great
ideas and a little bit of cash."

Subscription: $24.00/year (4 issues); sampler set of four back
issues, $16.50. Research Done Write!, Suite B261-TFE, 8726
S. Sepulveda Blvd., Los Angeles, CA 90045-4082; (310) 568-9861;
e-mail: KmberlyNLA@aol.com.

The Cheapskate Monthly, editor/publisher: Mary Hunt. This monthly
newsletter provides practical solutions, inspiration, and motivation
for individuals seeking debt-free living.

Subscription: $15.95/year (12 issues). Cheapskate Monthly,
PO Box 2135, Paramount, CA 90723-8135; (310) 630-8845;
(310) 630-3433 (fax); e-mail: Cheapsk8@ix.netcom.com.

Communication Briefings, editor: Jack Gillespie. A monthly idea
source filled with down-to-earth communication ideas and
techniques presented in digest form.

Subscription: $79.00/year (12 issues). Encoders, Inc., 1101 King
St., Suite 110, Alexandria, VA 22314; (703) 548-3800;
(703) 684-2136 (fax).

Guerrilla Marketing Newsletter, editor: Jay Conrad Levinson. Filled
with valuable advice, this newsletter presents practical tips and
insights on mastering the art of guerrilla marketing.

Subscription: $59.00/year (6 issues). Guerrilla Marketing
International, 260 Cascade Dr., Box 1336, Mill Valley, CA 94942;
(800) 748-6444; (415) 381-8361 (in California).

Living Cheap News, editor/publisher: Larry Roth. This newsletter promotes frugality as a way of life, offering inspirational and practical articles about various topics in each issue.

Subscription: $12.00/year (10 issues). Living Cheap Press, 7232 Belleview, Kansas City, MO 64114; (816) 523-3161; (816) 523-0224 (fax).

Newsletter News and Resources, editor/publisher: Elaine Floyd. A quarterly filled with tips and cost-cutting ideas for all areas of small business operation, especially focused on how to market with newsletters.

Subscription: $24.95/year (4 issues). Newsletter Resources, 6614 Pernod Ave., St. Louis, MO 63139; (314) 647-0400; (314) 647-1609 (fax).

The Penny Pincher, editor/publisher: Jackie Iglehart. This creative newsletter not only offers constructive ways to save, it also prints a tally at the end of each article of potential dollar savings if the ideas are used.

Subscription: $15.00/year (12 issues). The Penny Pincher, 2 Hilltop Rd., Mendham, NJ 07945-1215; (800) 41-PENNY.

The Pocket Change Investor, editors/publishers: Gerry Detweiler and Marc Eisenson. This quarterly publication helps consumers manage their debts, bills, taxes, and expenses, through well-researched frugal tips and strategies.

Subscription: $12.95/year (4 issues), $19.95 for two years (8 issues). Good Advice Press, Box 78, Elizaville, NY 12523; (800) 255-0899; (914) 758-1475 (fax).

Publishing Poynters, editor/publisher: Dan Poynter. Tips in an easy-to-digest paragraph format, covering all aspects of sales and marketing issues for independent publishers and small businesses.

For a free copy of the newsletter and an information kit on writing and publishing books, contact: Para Publishing, PO Box 8206-334, Santa Barbara, CA 93118-8206; (805) 968-7277; (805) 968-1379 (fax); e-mail: orders@parapublishing.com; http://www.parapublishing.com/books/para/334 (Internet).

The Skinflint Entrepreneur, editor/publisher: John Cali. This publication features frugal tidbits as well as a listing of money-saving products and services from other subscribers.

Subscription: $24.95/year (6 issues). Great Western Publishing Company, 21244 Millwood Square, Sterling, VA 20165-7607; (703) 404-0093; (703) 421-9542 (fax).

Index

Acknowledgments

Many individuals played a part in making *The Frugal Entrepreneur* a reality, and it is my pleasure to acknowledge them here. First, thanks to my two project assistants, Anne Allen and Katy Seaholm. Anne excelled in organizing the hundreds of bits of information in the book's early stages, while Katy's editorial eye helped to polish the material in its later form. Gratitude is extended, too, to Nancy Stabile, who always makes me marvel at how her skillful copyediting can clarify a thought and make a reader's experience more enjoyable.

Once again, I was pleased to have the talented designer Leslie Newman and her assistant Flora Wong as part of my publishing team. I learned long ago that words on a page remain lifeless (and unread!) without good design, and I know the icons and layout of this volume greatly contribute to its value. Appreciation is also extended to Michael Lonier of The Color Bureau for the Linotronic output.

Putting together *The Frugal Entrepreneur* reaffirmed my belief that entrepreneurs are among the most creative people on the planet these days, and I am fortunate to be able to work with so many of them on a regular basis. Special appreciation goes to fellow small business writers and consultants Lisa Aldisert, Jeff Berner, Barbara Brabec, Alice Bredin, Marianne Carroll, Jim Donovan, Jonathan Evetts, Paulette Ensign, David Garfinkel, Barbara Hemphill, Constance Hallinan Lagan, Ellen Leanse, Rebecca Morgan, Susan RoAne, Barrie Selack, Fred Showker, and Barbara Winter for sharing their dreams, schemes, joys, and challenges of life as an entrepreneur. Thanks, too, to the thousands of individuals who have participated in my seminars, and who continue to inspire me. Particular acknowledgment goes to the dozens of entrepreneurs who contributed ideas to this volume, listed on pages 155–156.

Entrepreneurial publishers are redefining the way information is created and shared in the late 1990s, and I'm grateful to be part of a network of colleagues who are pushing traditional boundaries and inventing new avenues of exchange. Hats off to Judy Byers, Ed Dudkowski, Elaine Floyd, Greg Godek, Larry Kesslin, John Kremer, Dan Poynter, Marilyn and Tom Ross, and Pippa Sales for creating innovative ways to share information with entrepreneurs— and for their generosity in offering feedback and support of Portico Press's publishing efforts. For the techno-wizardry of creating the Portico Press presence on the Internet in an easy-to-use way for the global community to access, my appreciation goes to Tim Celeski and Wayne Wong of Acme Media Moving & Storage in Seattle. Thanks, too, to Heather Cameron and the team at Publishers Group West for continuing to be an important partner in helping me serve entrepreneurs. A special note of appreciation to Susan Reich, who believed in this book when it was a mere glimmer of an idea jotted on a notepad.

Last, but certainly not least, I'm grateful to a special group of people who knew exactly when to ask, "How's the book coming?"—and when not to ask at all. To Bill and Yvonne Allenson, Marylyn Dintenfass, Susan Flynn, Gail Freedman, EddieLynn Morgan, Glenna Salsbury, David Tisdale, my family, and in particular my husband, Robert Sedestrom, I say: "Thanks for being part of the adventure. Now wait until you hear my *next* idea...."

Contributors

Successful entrepreneurs understand that when it comes to tackling a project, the more creative minds you can gather, the better the results. My thanks to the many frugal-minded entrepreneurs who submitted ideas for this collection. As a result of their contributions, *The Frugal Entrepreneur* is a much richer resource for entrepreneurs everywhere.

Anne Allen
New Paltz, NY

Markus Allen
Newtown Square, PA

Tom Antion
Landover Hills, MD

Dorrit Berg
New Paltz, NY

Irv Blackman
Chicago, IL

Wally Bock
Oakland, CA

Jason Brand
New City, NY

Judy Byers
Denver, CO

Nancy Castleman
Elizaville, NY

Victoria Chorbajian
River Edge, NJ

Ann Homer Cook
Jackson, MS

Sheila Delson
Poughkeepsie, NY

Kevin Donnalley
Burke, VA

Ed Dudkowski
Sausalito, CA

Marc Eisenson
Elizaville, NY

Paulette Ensign
Bedford Hills, NY

Lisa Fisher
Boston, MA

Elaine Floyd
St. Louis, MO

Jon Frost
West Pittston, PA

Chuck Galey
Jackson, MS

David Garfinkel
San Francisco, CA

Mary Beth Gehl
Pittsburgh, PA

Greg Godek
Weymouth, MA

Barbara Hemphill
Raleigh, NC

Ron Hertenstein
Fort Wayne, IN

Betty Hunter
Los Angeles, CA

Terri Kabachnick
Cromwell, CT

Kenneth Koubek
Weymouth, MA

Allison Kozak
Montgomery, NY

Constance Hallinan Lagan
North Babylon, NY

Edward D. Lekson
Columbus, OH

Mark McBride
Baton Rouge, LA

Rebecca Morgan
San Jose, CA

Kim Mosley
Ferguson, MO

Lucy Mundo
Livingston, NJ

Terry Paulson
Agoura Hills, CA

Polly Pattison
Westminster, CA

Maria Pearson
Boca Raton, FL

Odette Pollar
Oakland, CA

Dan Poynter
Santa Barbara, CA

Christine Puliselic
Winston-Salem, NC

Jim Rhode
Phoenix, AZ

Lillian Rojas
Branford, CT

Barbara Sacker
Brooklyn, NY

Fred Showker
Harrisonburg, VA

Nancy Stanich
New Paltz, NY

Alison Swerdloff
Lynbrook, NY

Steven Tavares
Pawcatuck, CT

David Tisdale
New York, NY

Neil Trager
New Paltz, NY

Carol Vincie
New York, NY

Robert Wagner
Kingston, NY

Howard Wolf
Palo Alto, CA

Sheila Zia
Ashland, OR

Let's Hear Your Frugal Ideas!

Submit your ideas to be included in
The Frugal Entrepreneur 2

We're starting to put together our next book of frugal-minded tips— and you're invited to take part! If your submission is selected, you'll receive a listing as a contributor, and an autographed copy of the book when it's published.

What creative ideas do you have to save time, energy, and money in your business? Send them along to us in any of three ways:

1) By e-mail: frugal@workingsolo.com

2) By fax: (914) 255-2116

3) By mail: Portico Press, PO Box 190, New Paltz NY 12561

Be sure to include your name, address, and daytime telephone number so that we can follow up with you.

We look forward to hearing your ideas!

Boost Your Business with Other Portico Press Resources

Discover the wide range of entrepreneurial tools created by self-employment expert Terri Lonier designed to help you boost your business profits.

BOOKS

Working Solo: The Real Guide to Freedom & Financial Success. This is the award-winning, easy-to-read classic that gives you a detailed road map for solo success. Named the #1 choice for solo entrepreneurs in an *Inc.* magazine cover story. 400 pages, $14.95.

Working Solo Sourcebook: Essential Resources for Independent Entrepreneurs. More than 1,200 valuable business resources, all gathered in one easy-to-use volume. Includes books, audios, services, supplies, professional networks and associations, and more. 320 pages, $14.95.

AUDIOTAPES

Working Solo: Getting Started. In an engaging, conversational format, Terri Lonier guides listeners through the opportunities and pitfalls facing new solo business owners. A great resource for solo newcomers or those ready to make the entrepreneurial leap. 2 cassettes, approx. 2 hours, $17.95.

Working Solo: Getting Customers. Packed with specific strategies and surefire techniques, this tape shows you how to generate a steady stream of customers for your company's products or services. 1 cassette, approx. 90 minutes, $12.95.
(Available after 1/97)

NEWSLETTER

The **Working Solo Newsletter** keeps you up to date on news, marketing ideas, legal and tax issues, solo management techniques, new products and services, and other valuable business information. Quarterly; subscriptions are $24.00/year.

INTERNET

Visit the **Working Solo Online** web site on the Internet at **http://www.workingsolo.com**, and explore a world of information on today's most dynamic business sector, self-employment. Receive updates on **Working Solo news and resources** by sending e-mail to info@workingsolo.com.

SEMINARS AND PRESENTATIONS

Terri Lonier is a professional speaker who gives seminars and presentations nationwide on entrepreneurial topics. If you would like to have Terri speak to or consult for your company or organization, or to attend one of her seminars, contact her by e-mail at: soloexpert@workingsolo.com.

To Order

Working Solo books and audiotapes can be found in bookstores nationwide, and all products can be ordered directly from the **Working Solo Order Desk** at **(800) 222-SOLO.**

Portico Press books and audios are available to the bookstore trade through Publishers Group West at (800) 788-3123, or from Ingram, Baker & Taylor, and other fine wholesalers.

Quantity orders and discount information can be found on page 6.

To buy additional copies of the *The Frugal Entrepreneur* or other Portico Press information resources, visit your local bookstore or photocopy the order form below.

ORDER FORM

Four convenient ways to order:

By phone: Call (800) 222-SOLO (orders only)
Please have your Visa, AmEx or MasterCard ready.

By fax: (914) 255-2116 (24 hours a day)

By mail: Portico Press
PO Box 190
New Paltz, NY 12561-0190
(914) 255-7165

By e-mail: portico@workingsolo.com

Please send me:

_____ copies of *The Frugal Entrepreneur* @ $12.95

_____ copies of *Working Solo* @ $14.95

_____ copies of the *Working Solo Audio* @ $17.95

_____ copies of the *Working Solo Sourcebook*

_____ Paperback @ $14.95   _____ Hardcover @ $24.95

Name _____

Address _____

City/State/Zip _____

Daytime Phone _____

Sales Tax:
Please add 7.75% sales tax to the total order for books shipped to New York State addresses.

Shipping:
$3.00 for the first item and $1.00 for each additional item.

Payment Method:
_____Check   _____Visa   _____MasterCard   _____American Express

Card Number _____

Name on card _____ Exp. date: _____/_____